Your Towns and Cities in the ...

Doncaster
in the Great War

Your Towns and Cities in the Great War

Doncaster
in the Great War

Symeon Mark Waller

Pen & Sword
MILITARY

First published in Great Britain in 2014 by
PEN & SWORD MILITARY
an imprint of
Pen and Sword Books Ltd
47 Church Street
Barnsley
South Yorkshire S70 2AS

ISBN 978 1 78303 644 8

Printed and bound in England
by CPI Group (UK) Ltd, Croydon, CR0 4YY

Typeset in Times New Roman by Chic Graphics

Pen & Sword Books Ltd incorporates the imprints of
Pen & Sword Archaeology, Atlas, Aviation, Battleground, Discovery,
Family History, History, Maritime, Military, Naval, Politics, Railways,
Select, Social History, Transport, True Crime, and Claymore Press,
Frontline Books, Leo Cooper, Praetorian Press, Remember When,
Seaforth Publishing and Wharncliffe.

For a complete list of Pen and Sword titles please contact
Pen and Sword Books Limited
47 Church Street, Barnsley, South Yorkshire, S70 2AS, England
E-mail: enquiries@pen-and-sword.co.uk
Website: www.pen-and-sword.co.uk

Contents

Acknowledgements

With grateful thanks to the Doncaster Library Service for allowing me access to the *Doncaster Chronicle* and *Doncaster Gazette* newspapers.

To Margaret Bowen for her hard work in proof-reading and spell-checking.

A special thank you to Harrison and Eunice Ball for the use of the pictures of items in their personal collection. These items proved to be an invaluable source of inspiration to me as I struggled to get into the mindset of the fighting soldier.

And to my wife for her patience and understanding during the writing of this book.

Introduction

Over the centuries the people occupying the settlement of Doncaster have played a part in defending the country from one foe or another.

During the time of the Saxons there were conflicts between kingdoms. Along came the Normans with various bloody engagements during the Harrying of the North. The town was a hive of excitement, trepidation and confusion during the Wars of the Roses in the fifteenth century. Conisbrough Castle was a base for the ill-fated Richard, Duke of York, and it was from here that he set out for his property at Sandal Castle and the Battle of Wakefield where he was defeated and killed by Lancastrian supporters of King Henry VI.

Fast forward to the seventeenth century and townsfolk were called to choose between the Crown or Cromwell in the English Civil War. The civil conflict of that period caused much disturbance as armies marched along the Great North Road from north to south and back again. Cromwell and his men arrived in Doncaster to be entertained by the Corporation at the expense of the townspeople. That both the King's men and Parliamentarians came to Doncaster in search of new recruits is well documented.

As the Victorian period was ending, came the Boer War with its improved fire power through advancing technology. At its end in 1902 the wounded arrived back on our shores and Doncaster families lamented their sons who had fallen on African soil. The dust settled, peace and tranquillity returned and Doncaster slipped back into its routine as an emerging mining town. Relative normality resumed and the memories of war gradually faded.

The harmony ended abruptly in the mid-summer of 1914 when the Great War erupted in Europe. Once again Doncaster men and boys were called to arms and Doncaster felt the sadness and anguish that can only come when those that are dearest to us are laying their lives on the line. Doncastrians, it seems, were a willing bunch when it came to fighting for what they were persuaded to believe was a good cause.

However, in the long years of war Doncaster was shaken to its foundations and communities were damaged beyond repair. People's memories of the Great War still persisted into the twenty-first century but with the 100th anniversary these have all but faded away.

This book looks at ways in which the First World War took its toll on Doncaster in particular. It serves, not only as a lasting memory for a generation in danger of forgetting, but also, and more importantly, as a means of expressing grateful recognition for the men and boys who lost their lives in that conflict.

Symeon Mark Waller

CHAPTER 1

Peace is Shattered

August bank holiday has become a time of year that is looked forward to by many, much the same as Christmas and Easter, for it is a time of rest and relaxation and a time for family reunions after a year of work. It would be a time of sunny seaside excursions and picnics in the countryside if it were not for our ever-changing and unpredictable climate making it harder and harder to plan for these things. This period of mid-summer recuperation has been a tradition for a great many years. My grandmother recalls with fondness her annual day trip to Skegness with her peers as the focal point of the whole year! She remembers those trips with that bright sunny memory that we all possess when we romance about the happiest moments from our childhood. She was born in 1925 to Isaac and Eliza Brookes sharing a small, three-bedroom pit-house on Rostholme Square in Bentley, firstly with her elder sister Joyce, and then closely followed by another sister and four brothers. Although her memory of daily life is ebbing away she holds tightly to those halcyon days spent chasing waves on Skegness beach.

On the approach to August bank holiday in 1913 things were not much different to those of previous years. In Doncaster, mining was in its heyday. Men and boys worked long hours down the 'pit', while women and daughters were busy keeping a home clean and tidy and preparing simple and affordable meals. One advertisement which appeared in the local newspaper was tailored specifically for those working hard in the kitchen at home, it reads:

'EVERY HOUSEWIFE IS HER OWN FOOD CONTROLLER
- You can make an endless variety of milk puddings, savouries,
baked puddings, etc with "Atora Shredded Suet" and the rice,
flaked maize, oatmeal, lentils, peas, beans, etc advised by the
Food Ministry for saving wheat flour. "Atora" makes puddings
very light and very nourishing. Fritters made of these cereals
should be fried in "Atora Block Suet". "Atora" is sold by all
grocers in 1lb boxes for 1s. 5d. or ½lb boxes for 9d.'

Life was hard with no support from the government to prop up the
family unit in times of financial difficulty. Illnesses which are now
common and curable were proving fatal. According to the census
returns of 1911, it was not uncommon for a family to lose more than
one child in infancy so that eight or more babies might have been born
in order to arrive at the typical family of four.

WOODLANDS
SPORTS AND SHOW,

BANK HOLIDAY
(4th AUGUST).

GATES OPEN 12-30.

BRODSWORTH MAIN
versus
BULLCROFT MAIN.
WICKETS PITCHED ONE O'CLOCK

SPORTS START TWO O'CLOCK.

STEADMAN'S MOTORS RUN DIRECT
TO THE GROUND FROM FRENCH
GATE.

According to the *Doncaster Gazette* of 1 August 1913 the challenges of day-to-day life were being met quite normally as they always had. The mining community in the village of Woodlands were to have their annual 'Sports and Show', a cricket match between their own Brodsworth Main Colliery and Bullcroft Main Colliery in Carcroft. The event began at 2pm with Steadman's Motors providing the transport from French Gate in Doncaster to the cricket ground in Woodlands. In nearby Bentley on 7 August, Lady Mary Cooke opened a garden sale in the grounds of St Peter's Vicarage in aid of the Parish Room Building Fund, with tickets 6d each. In the town centre jobs were being advertised. A.G. Dover of Silver Street, Doncaster, was in need of a Junior Assistant with knowledge of outfitting and tailoring, whilst the West Riding National Insurance Committee of Camden Street required a Clerk to the District Committee to work for £30 per annum.

Men were getting married and women being given in marriage. Even clergy were tying the knot, for in the first days of August, the Reverend Percy Ineson of the Wesleyan Chapel in Bentley, was betrothed to Edith Fanny Perkins. The mines needed miners and the miners needed houses which led to many fields and open spaces being turned over to the property developer. In Toll Bar, just north of Bentley, Arthur De Burgh of York was offering land for sale for this very purpose. An advert in the *Doncaster Gazette* reads:

'BUILDERS, CONTRACTORS AND MANUFACTURERS
Hall Villa Estates, of Askern Road, Bentley is within easy distance of four new collieries. Having sold a large School Site to the West Riding County Council, I am now offering BUILDING PLOTS (any size) adjoining the School Site on reasonable terms. Would entertain exchange for house property. The estate has a frontage to the Hull and Barnsley Railway of over 500 yards so offers exceptional sites for factories etc. Allotments (any size) for gardens, poultry, pig keeping, etc. at reasonable rentals.'

Civic pride was at its height and a deep love for King and Country was ever-present. A unity was felt between families, communities and regions that was unbreakable and people looked back with pride to past victories like Trafalgar and Waterloo, chronologically as equidistant from that decisive battle as we now are from the Great War. We were a nation to be feared (or so we thought) and those victories led us to suppose that we were invincible. We were clearly not, as the years to come would reveal.

One hundred years have passed since the outbreak of the First World War. The last remaining veterans have passed away and the only accounts we have now are second-hand. No longer do our grandfathers furnish us with the realities of that war so that the whole bloody mess has developed into a tradition rather than a reality. In 1913, Doncaster folk were in a similar position. The legacy of the Napoleonic Wars was one of victorious rejoicing. Men and boys were under the false impression that any attempt by our European cousins to upset our tranquillity would prove fruitless. We were not afraid of confrontation; we were a super-power not to be under-estimated.

We had a local army regiment too in the form of the 4th and 5th Battalions of the King's Own Yorkshire Light Infantry with headquarters at Pontefract, the ranks of which were largely raised from Doncaster and Wakefield. In August 1913 the battalions were enjoying themselves in Wales for the bank holiday under the pretence of 'training'. The newspaper headline read:

'CAMP BY THE SEA - Local Territorials at Aberystwyth, 9,000 men under canvas'.

The 5th King's Own Yorkshire Light Infantry, or the KOYLI as they were affectionately known, had left their families in late July to embark on their usual fortnight of training under the leadership of Colonel C.C. Moxon and Major Archer. They were going to take their place in the 3rd West Riding Brigade, forming part of the West Yorkshire Division, our town being represented by 25 officers and 673 men. A far cry from the suffering and intensity of the battlefields, the camp grounds were beautifully situated among the romantic hills which overlooked the picturesque town. An account of the first days of training was in the *Doncaster Gazette* of 31 July 1913:

'After a long, hot and tiring journey on Sunday, the sleeping soldiers were rudely awakened at 5.30 on Monday morning. It was a glorious sunrise and even camp duties seemed a pleasure in the brilliant sunshine and the fresh air of daybreak. By the time breakfast was over and the men were paraded ready for marching off, the heat was increasing, and with the breeze of the morning dying down to nothing, it became very hot. The drill and manoeuvre areas are 4 miles from the camps and the roads are narrow, rough, and steep. This 8-mile march to and from the scene of action is an unwelcome addition to the day's work.

'The plan adopted is to put in a good morning's work, get back to camp around two o'clock, and then take it easy for the rest of the day, filling in the time with lectures on the care of arms, outpost duties, and the necessary inspections of arms and kit. This plan will be departed from next week, when the troops will be taken up on to the hills for brigade and divisional movements, and will be absent from camp two days at a time. No better country for the training of troops could be found than these Welsh uplands. In the vast spaces there is plenty of room for every exercise, and in such variety of country experience, all kinds of cover and distance-judging can be obtained. Modern warfare is very largely a game of "hide and seek", and that game can be played to perfection in the deep gullies and broken ground of the mountain sides.'

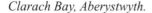

Clarach Bay, Aberystwyth.

Lance-Corporal W. H. Brunt of the QOYD, in France.

There is no doubt that the men were being trained to within an inch of their lives, but what better surroundings in which to learn. Within easy reach of the camp was Clarach Bay with its stretch of beautiful, fine sand and the blue water of Cardigan Bay. In the afternoons it received the bodies of thousands of perspiring warriors who emerged from its vastness brighter and better men.

Other regiments of the British Army recruited locally including the Queen's Own Yorkshire Dragoons which took a great many men from Doncaster into battle.

The training camps, manoeuvres, drills and exercises soon came to an end so that, by the middle of August 1913, the soldiers were back with their families enjoying what was left of the summer.

Christmas approached and as the temperatures decreased the children of Doncaster, like coiled springs, enjoyed the excitement of that magical time of year. The whole town got into the spirit of the season with the Great Northern Railway Company organising 'Express Christmas Excursions from Doncaster'. Breaks of 3, 4, 6, or 15 days were advertised taking in the Eastern Counties, Nottingham, Leeds, Bradford, Dewsbury and London. A 'Christmas Eve Dance' was promised – Mr J.R. Gascoigne's 'Sixth Annual Confetti Cinderella Dance' to be held in the New Trades Institute. Dancing was from 8pm until midnight, with refreshments at reasonable charges and an on-the-door ticket price of 5/-, or for the younger reader, 5 shillings. And, if you were short of Christmas gift ideas, then 'Goodlys' of 18 and 20 Station Road, Doncaster declared:

'Get ready for Christmas and brighten your home with extra comforts. Goodlys Doncaster Furnishing Company has excellent lines in Easy Chairs, Carpets, all kinds of Furniture, and other home requirements at the lowest prices! Also scores of suitable goods for gifts which include, Slipper Boxes, Palm Stands, Easy Chairs, Trinket and Toilet sets, Cushions and Rugs to name a few. Presents priced from 2/- to £5'.

There was even an advertisement for workers at the brand new coal mine at Edlington posted in the *Gazette* of 3 December 1913 for 'Yorkshire Main Colliery' which read, 'Wanted, 200 Colliers'. With the wage paid being from 8 shillings and three pence to 9 shillings per shift, an average worker could expect to provide their families with an extra £2 per week (after paying Messrs. Steadman and Sons their 5 shilling motor-charabanc fee), a welcome amount of money for any struggling Doncaster family at this time of year!

Advert from 1913 Doncaster Gazette.

As good a Christmas as any was had by the townsfolk of Doncaster in 1913 and rightly so for they had worked extremely hard for it all year round. The year 1914 was upon them and work and school resumed. Fathers went back to the mines and boys followed close behind. Mothers washed, ironed, cooked and cleaned with their daughters in tow, learning the ropes.

As the cold winter months gave way to the warm winds of springtime and the crocuses and cherry blossom bade farewell for another year, the summer arrived in Doncaster at long last. Completely oblivious to the compounding tensions overseas, the town and its people worked and played the same as ever. The miners at Bentley colliery enjoyed breaking records as 285 tonnes of coal was wound to the surface every hour for the first eight hours of the shift on Monday, 27 April 1914. Messrs Hodgson and Hepworth were served with an order to quit their premises on St Sepulchre Gate in the town to make way for the street widening scheme.

Not too far away, notices were served on the owners of Milner's Yard, off French Gate, but for a completely different reason. At a meeting of the Sanitary Committee, the Sanitary Inspector reported upon the condition of eleven houses in the yard saying, 'they are not in a reasonably habitable condition', and so closing orders were served on the owners of the properties. The Army Stores at 36 Printing Office Street advertised discounted rates on stock for 'the working man', with army boots and territorial's boots reduced to 5 shillings per pair - did they have inside information perhaps?

The Doncaster Gazette, shortly before the war began, had this newsworthy item for the people of the town: Second Lieutenant G.C. Whitaker, who joined the 5th Battalion of the King's Own Yorkshire

_._.... .nfantry in January 1913, had resigned his post with immediate effect. Had he been following the proceedings in Europe and favoured a back-seat view?

Meanwhile, the Queen's Own Yorkshire Dragoons, that other local regiment, had arrived back from their training camp in Scarborough without knowing how soon their knowledge was going to be needed. With the benefit of hindsight we can see how that quality training was indeed 'food at the proper time'. Of the instructional period on the North Yorkshire coastline, it was said:

> 'The tactical exercises have been carried out with keenness and intelligence, and the men have shown a thorough interest in their arduous work. General Plumer, after his inspection, wrote and spoke of the smartness of the men and the general excellence of the horses. The Brigadier, Colonel Nickall, who spent much time in the camp, was also appreciative of the way that the men conducted themselves during their time at Scarborough, and the Commanding Officer, Colonel W. McKenzie-Smith, stated that 'he was well pleased with all ranks', and it had been gratifying for him to hear from leading residents in the town tributes to the general good conduct and smartness of the men. The men had begun to leave camp at 7 o'clock on Saturday morning and those of the Doncaster Squadron arrived home early in the afternoon.'

How lucky for these men to have undergone so successful a training mission and so close to the outbreak of the war, for not six weeks later on 28 June 1914, the heir to the Austrian Empire, Franz Ferdinand, was visiting Sarajevo, the capital of Bosnia, with his wife. Tensions were already high in this part of the world and it was an extremely unwise move for the Austrian heir to have graced the people with his presence. Bosnia was keen to detach itself from the governance of Austria and to join forces with neighbouring Serbia to become a new 'independent' state. The Austrian presence of Franz Ferdinand was too much for certain members of the Bosnian society to bear and they assassinated Ferdinand and his wife.

What happened next was the beginning of what we now call World War One. A cataclysmic eruption of ill feeling and mass hysteria throughout the whole world as nations united and revolted in a bloody

The Queen's Own Yorkshire Dragoons on Scarborough Beach.

battle that was to last four years. On 5 July 1914, the Germans vowed to back Austria in their fight against Serbia which Austria declared on 28 July. On 1 August, Germany declared war on Russia, and two days later on France, before invading Belgium. Then, on 4 August 1914, Great Britain declared war on Germany.

The people of Doncaster were in the war whether they liked it or not and, far from being a normal year of typical Yorkshire life, this year was to unfold into a life-changing epoch so catastrophic that its events would be passionately recalled on into the twenty-first century.

CHAPTER 2

Eager for a Fight

How did Doncaster take the news? The town had only just begun to get over the Boer Wars. Was this new European focus a welcome return to the arenas of war for those men who had returned from Africa unscathed?

It seems the mood was one of eager anticipation. The *Gazette* headlines read:

DONCASTER AND THE WAR - EFFECTS ON THE TOWN AND NEIGHBOURHOOD - UNPARALLELED SCENES OF EXCITEMENT!

It took the people of Doncaster one or two days to gather the full import of the events which were occurring with such cumulative rapidity on the Continent and in London. The latest telegraph messages of the advancements in Europe were posted in the windows of the *Doncaster Gazette* newspaper office. The message boards created the keenest of interest with what seemed like most of the town's men paying the windows a visit, so that by the Sunday after Britain's part in the war was declared, where there would have normally been an air of silent calm around the town, there was now heard the ear-piercing cry of the newspaper sellers at their stands from almost every street corner, both in the town centre and in the suburbs. One or two of the evening papers had even issued special 'war editions'. The railway station at Doncaster became a focal point of the proceedings too as large numbers of the Royal Naval Reserve passed through the station followed by more of the blue-clad men waiting to board trains on the platforms. Territorial soldiers were also on the move, in some cases men who had only proceeded to their training grounds on the previous day had been recalled to active service before they had settled down to the daily routine of camp life.

The Doncaster Territorials were about to start their second week of training at a camp at Whitby, North Yorkshire, when the news came for them to pack up and come home. Just after the 7am breakfast on Monday, 10 August, the call came from the War Office and before too long, in orderly fashion and without undue commotion, the tents, supplies and equipment were being packed away in preparation for the hasty retreat to Doncaster. The whole process of breaking camp took only four hours after which the dinner rations were handed out. The companies were formed up and were briefly addressed by the Brigadier, Colonel Dawson, who explained to them the true reason for their return to Doncaster. There must have been mixed emotions in the Whitby field that day.

Scenes that were closely akin to the first symptoms of war fever were witnessed at Whitby station that afternoon. The company bands played as the troops filed onto the platforms where a number of special trains had been chartered for their conveyance. A large crowd had assembled on the square in front of the station to cheer on the Territorials as they rounded the corner from the hill that led to their camp.

The Doncaster men arrived at their headquarters about 1am on Tuesday morning, after which time the Drill Hall in French Gate was the main centre of all the excitement with which the town had been seething. A constant crowd of curious spectators watched the comings and goings of officers and messengers. On Wednesday, 12 August the mobilisation of the Queen's Own Yorkshire Dragoons commenced, giving Doncaster the appearance of a military town rather than of a fairly busy industrial centre. Over the next few days Doncaster was to take on this military appearance to a greater degree as the immediate surrounding area had been chosen as a 'War Centre'.

It was soon invaded by the West Riding Division and opened its doors to several thousand infantry and artillery men. The Guild Hall, the Free Library, St George's School and the Vicarage were converted into accommodation for the soldiers and, eventually, it was planned for all of the borough schools to be utilised for this purpose. Many of the town's householders received notices calling upon them to billet the men, and several of the officers of the West Riding Division visited Doncaster to complete the accommodation arrangements. The Queen's Own Yorkshire Dragoons' sleeping quarters for the first few days were the stands at the racecourse, such was the urgency and shortage of proper accommodation.

Special arrangements were made for the reception and dispatch of the thousands of troops entering and leaving Doncaster in the form of a temporary platform which was constructed in the sidings just outside the main Doncaster railway station. Among the first Doncaster folk to be called up for active service was Mr G.C. Venn, one of the assistants at the Divisional office who was a Naval Reservist, and who left on Saturday, 8 August to be with the Fleet.

Amidst all the confusion of regiments returning, soldiers just passing through, officers being re-called, and new recruits offering their services, little thought was given to those members of the family who were to be left behind. Some of the men and boys had only just returned from their training and their wives and children, who had been eagerly awaiting their return, had been left with an empty void as their loved ones were paraded in front of them before being whisked away to Europe. The following eyewitness statement of a scene outside Doncaster station illustrates perfectly the sadness that was felt across the town, for it reads:

'On Wednesday morning, outside Doncaster station, stood a woman, bare-headed, holding in her arms a small child, staring through her tears blankly into space. "Where's Daddy gone?" piped the baby in a plaintive note. The answer was a fresh outburst of tears for Daddy had gone to Manchester to rejoin his regiment. The tear-stained woman was not alone, but perhaps the amazing part of the trend of events this week has been the phlegmatic indifference, and even the light-heartedness of both soldiers and civilians in Doncaster.' - Anon.

The Doncaster Grand Theatre, which today stands forlorn amidst a sea of twenty-first century development, was commandeered by the military authorities for billeting purposes. Even two members of the

Recruiting soldiers at Equity Chambers, High Street, Doncaster..

cast of 'Australian Nell', the show that was being acted out at the 'Grand' that very week, were called away as Army Reservists. The Palace Theatre too lost one or two of its artistes who were either Naval or Army Reserve men. Right across the borough, men were being plucked from their jobs and families and whisked back to their regimental headquarters to join the war effort in Europe. A long-running advertisement that became a regular feature in Doncaster's newspapers was a government call which contained the following message:

> 'Temporary Commissions in His Majesty's Army - 2,000 Junior Officers (un-married) are immediately required in consequence

of the increase of the regular army. Terms of Service - To serve with the Regular Army until the War is concluded. Age 17 to 30. An allowance of £20 will be made for uniform and of £5.15 shillings for equipment. How you can obtain his Majesty's Commission: Cadets or ex-Cadets of the University Training Corps or members of a University should apply to their commanding officers or to the authorities of their University. Other young men of good general education should apply in person to the Officer commanding the nearest depot. Full information can be obtained by written application to the secretary, War Office. GOD SAVE THE KING.'

Colonel S.E. Somerville requested that all men who had previously served in the Regular Army, Royal Navy, Special Reserve, Militia, Territorial Force and Volunteers were to give in their names at once at the headquarters of the Doncaster Battalion of the National Reserve, which was based at 'Equity Chambers', 55 High Street, Doncaster. No man was exempt from service of one form or another, even men to whom the government had issued certificates of ill health had them revoked, much to their dismay.

Within a matter of weeks, or even days, the War Office had more recruits than they could arm, equip, or properly train, and the new battalions drilled in plain clothes with dummy rifles or sticks under time-expired officers and NCOs and lived under canvas or billets wherever room could be found. Lord Kitchener, the Secretary of State for War, believed the Territorials to be somewhat of a liability, calling them 'Saturday afternoon soldiers'. It is a stigma that attached to the Territorial Army during that time and on into the future. Kitchener believed that they carried with them bad habits which were difficult for them to forget, habits that had served them well in previous wars but which would not be beneficial for them to practise in the modern methods of warfare that they now faced in Europe. The new recruits, who had no bad habits to forget, were quickly formed into their own battalions before being grafted on to the regular army, in this case the King's Own Yorkshire Light Infantry, so that by the end of 1914 the KOYLI consisted of twelve battalions.

The 2/4th and the 2/5th battalions of the KOYLI were predominantly raised in the Doncaster and Wakefield districts, their

SS Buteshire.

headquarters being at Pontefract. These reserves were originally created to act as supply battalions to the main 4th and 5th KOYLI but, as time went on and the country became more desperate for men, the reserve battalions would also see front line service. The 2nd KOYLI were mobilised in Dublin making them the first battalion to see active service in the Great War. They were amalgamated with the 2nd battalion of the King's Own Scottish Borderers, the 2nd battalion Duke of Wellington's West Riding Regiment, and the 1st Battalion Queen's Own Royal West Kent Regiment to form 13 Infantry Brigade under Brigadier General G.L. Cuthbert. How odd it must have seemed for the men to be suddenly merged with complete strangers from all over the country.

They sailed from Dublin on Friday, 14 August 1914 on board the SS *Buteshire*, arriving at Le Havre, on the River Seine estuary during the evening of Sunday, 16 August. From there they boarded trains bound for Maroilles on the Western Front, where they were to join the rest of 13 Infantry Brigade. From Sunday to Thursday of that week the men got to know each other. Little did they know that they would be fighting back to back in the not too distant future. On Thursday, 20 August General Sir Charles Fergusson, commander of the 5th Division of the Regular Army, addressed the men of the newly formed 13 Infantry Brigade saying, 'There must be no surrender, men must fight to the last with their fists if their rifles are useless; this will be a war of self-sacrifice; possibly whole battalions, even brigades, may have to be sacrificed in order to make it good for others.'

Certainly, the men were quick to answer the call to arms, they were eager to defend British soil, but were they ready to lay down their lives for the good of their neighbour? Time would tell.

The purpose of this book was never to give a minute-by-minute catalogue of events on the front lines as other books already do this. These pages are to tell the story of how the actions of the soldiers fighting abroad had a direct impact on Doncaster itself. However, I can go no further with this chapter without mentioning the gallantry that was displayed by the King's Own Yorkshire Light Infantry beginning on Sunday, 23 August on the line of the Mons-Condé Canal.

While the men were eating their meals the enemy advanced with a battery of field guns. Despite efforts to keep the Germans at bay, the onslaught was too strong and the enemy too formidable to hold any ground here. The order was given to fall back and this act and the operations that followed have become known to history as the Retreat from Mons. The welcome news for the troops was to be short lived for 2nd KOYLI as General Smith-Dorrien, against his superior's orders, turned to fight at Le Cateau and the battalion took up defensive positions to face the oncoming German strength.

One needs to read between the lines at this juncture to establish the reasons for the decision being made to fight rather than retreat. To refer to the words of Sir Charles Fergusson when he addressed his newly formed 13 Brigade, which included a KOYLI battalion, on 20 August, 'whole battalions may have to be sacrificed in order to make it good for others'. Smith-Dorrien had the experience and foresight to discern that if he could hold off, if only temporarily, the advancing German Army, then it would give the rest of the British Army who were flanking them at Mons, but now retreating to the Marne ahead of them, the chance to escape. And so the decision was not taken lightly, but made 'to make it good for others', self-sacrifice indeed!

Here we should mention the valour of one of Doncaster's own. George Henry Wyatt, although not an indigenous Doncastrian, was to settle in the town after the war and ascend the ranks of the borough police force to sergeant. On 25 August 1914 during the retreat 27-year-old Wyatt and his comrades were attempting to hold their position

G.H. Wyatt VC.

inside a cluster of farm buildings at Landrecies, not far from the French/Belgian border. They were under heavy fire as the enemy tried everything to gain entrance to the stronghold. A number of straw bales were set alight at the side of the buildings which threatened the position. Wyatt broke cover and ran to extinguish the flames in full view of the enemy. After two attempts he succeeded in his efforts while bullets were ricocheting all around him, allowing for the position to be maintained. Within days he went on to receive a severe head wound but only stopped fighting when the blood temporarily blinded him. For his bravery for the good of his fellows and in the face of extreme danger he was awarded the Victoria Cross, the highest award for gallantry for British and Commonwealth forces. He lived a happy and fulfilled life in Doncaster, earning the respect of the townsfolk, until his retirement in 1934. He died on 22 January 1964, aged 77, and is buried in Cadeby churchyard with his wife, Ellen.

At 6am on Tuesday, 25 August, the Brigade Commander sent orders which read: 'Orders have been changed. There will now be NO retirement for the fighting troops; fill up your trenches with water, food and ammunition as far as you can.' Messengers were sent with copies of this order to the companies and the order was communicated directly to the men in the trenches. The battalion ammunition reserve was sent for and dumped from the carts on the ground alongside battalion headquarters. The German batteries were already beginning to find their ranges on all visible objects. The boxes of ammunition were distributed by the buglers and the ground was rapidly cleared for action before the oncoming storm of shell. For the whole day on Wednesday, 26 August 1914, the King's Own Yorkshire Light Infantry fought hard to hold on to the ground where they stood. The forward companies of the KOYLI had used most, if not all, of their ammunition; the battalion reserve ammunition that had been so hurriedly deposited earlier had been exhausted and there was no possibility of any of the Reserve Brigade arriving on the scene to help. Finally, having held off the German attackers for long enough, the order came to retreat but for many it was already too late, they were as good as dead. Without food, water or ammunition, there was nothing for them to do but to stay and fight and die where they stood. The official history explains:

'For the last hour of the fight, so far as they could see, the KOYLI were alone in the line to stem the German advance; it was conceived that their duty lay in blocking the great high road and in denying it until the last possible minute to the enemy. Though their troops surrounded 2 KOYLI on three sides, completely dominating their flanks, and were supported by field guns brought up to within 900 yards of the trenches, the Germans still hesitated to rush in. Time after time their bugles sounded the British "Cease Fire" and attempts were made to send forward a flag of truce. Each overture was answered with bursts of fire and the remnants of the companies made it evident to the enemy that the resistance was being maintained... .

'The left companies' trenches were already overrun; the fire of the attack was closer and even more intense; when suddenly the whole countryside, as far as the eye could reach from right to left, seemed alive with advancing Germans. Major Yate shouted to our men to charge but was instantly afterwards struggling in the hands of the Germans who had approached from behind... . There was no surrender. The occupants of the trenches were mobbed and swamped by the rising tide of grey-coated Germans.

Private A. Brookes.

'The Battalion Headquarters trench was from its position naturally the last to be overrun. The amount of resistance any company was capable of offering at the last moment may be gauged from the fact that on the day following the battle, a British officer prisoner-of-war, on his way down the road under escort, counted sixty-two dead in the trenches by the side of the road alone. And this was after all the wounded had been accounted for. The other companies had suffered no less severely.'

According to the official statistics, the losses of the KOYLI at Le Cateau were 18 officers, 21 sergeants, 22 corporals, 7 buglers, and 532 privates, making a total of 600 men.

Sir Charles Fergusson reappeared again, this time with a different message:

'I am only too pleased to do anything in my power to recognise the behaviour of the battalion. It was mainly thanks to them that the II Corps was extricated that day, and their stand is historic... .'

The *Doncaster Chronicle* of 4 September 1914 allows one man the opportunity to tell the story in his own words. From the article entitled 'Battlefield Stories' we read:

'DONCASTER MAN'S EXPERIENCE AT MONS, In The Thick Of The Fight - Weird night ride with the wounded'.

'Private A. Brookes, of 46, Union Street, St Sepulchre Gate, to whom we are indebted for these details, and whose photograph we reproduce, though young in years, is an old soldier, and a typical one at that. He joined the Army, the KOYLI, second battalion, in 1907... , and finished his contracted service in May of this year. Questioned as to where he had been and what had happened since he was recalled to his regiment on 5 August 1914, Private Brookes said, "We were first removed to Dublin. On the 16th we were ordered on board ship and left for an unknown destination, and the next time we set foot on land it was in France. For a whole week after that we were marching across country. We were treated splendidly by the French people and had a glorious time, for they allowed us to want for nothing, and we could have anything we liked for the asking. We eventually arrived at a village called 'Boussu', and were there accommodated in a brewery. That was on a Saturday afternoon, and it was here that the regiment first came into contact with the enemy. Little did we know on that Saturday afternoon that we were only about a quarter of a mile from the enemy, but our officers must have gleaned some knowledge of their close proximity, and we were removed to a place a few hundred yards distant.

'Exactly as half past twelve chimed on Sunday afternoon the Germans "kicked off" and shells began to fall thick and fast around us. We had with us the King's Own Scottish Borderers, the East Surreys, the Royal Engineers and also a battery of artillery. The Germans were vastly superior in numbers, but we continued to give battle to them until 10 o'clock, when we received the order to retreat. It was a warm time I tell you, and we lost heavily, particularly the Borderers. The German losses must have been enormous. The order to retreat was obeyed, of course, but our fellows would have much preferred to have gone for the Germans. The Germans were always very prompt at 'kicking off', and fighting again started at daybreak on Monday morning, continuing until midday, when the order was again given to fall back. All that afternoon we were followed by aeroplanes. It was a hard time for us, and all we had to eat was what we set out with when we first gave way before the Germans.

'That night we got a little rest and also received some good food. It was easy to see that something big was going to happen soon as we were joined by thousands of other troops. On Tuesday night about 29 aeroplanes, apparently British, were flying overhead, and on the following morning we were ordered to dig trenches where we lay full length on the ground. At half-past six the enemy let us know they were there and there ensued a terrible struggle, now known to us as the Battle of Mons. It was a bloody struggle, and in the end we once more gave way.

'You can guess on the Germans method of advance when I tell you that it was only a matter of loading your rifle and firing as rapidly as you could. It was impossible to miss. They were packed like herrings in a box and as fast as one went down others appeared as though out of the very ground. Give me a rifle and a supply of ammunition and I could lay within a couple of hundred yards of a German company and feel as comfortable as I am now, but their artillery men were really fine at finding their range, assisted by their aviators, they could find us in next to no time.'

Reverting to the battle already described, Private Brookes said,

'As we were retiring I was shot through the first finger and the thumb, and later was injured in the fleshy part of the leg by a piece of shrapnel. Eventually, I succeeded, after losing my rifle and everything else, in reaching a Red Cross motor wagon, so full of wounded, however, that I was compelled to ride on the bonnet at the front. In this manner I rode from 5 o'clock in the evening until 7 o'clock the next morning when St Quentin was reached. Having been attended to there and also at the hospital at Havre, where we were also fed, we left on Friday night for

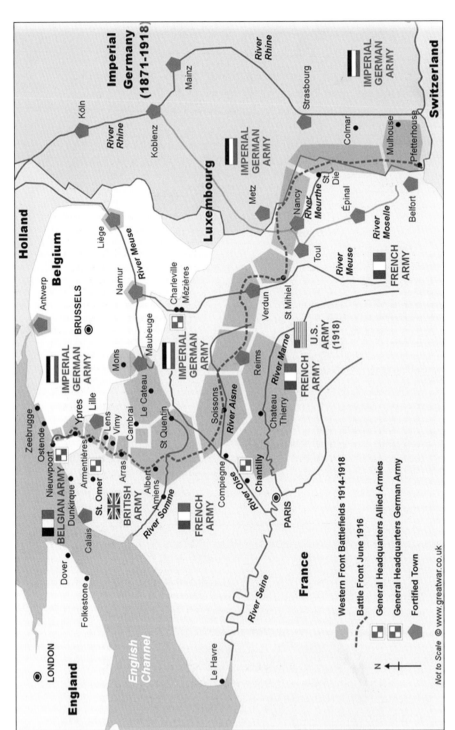

Battlefield Map

Southampton which was reached early on Saturday morning. From there I was taken to Netley Hospital close by, and was detained there until Friday, when I returned home to Doncaster.'

The temper of our men at the Front is easily gauged by some of the amusing incidents reported from time to time. Private Brookes tells of one such incident:

'A corporal and two men had a sweepstake as to who should "wing" the first German. Suddenly seven of the enemy appeared round a corner, and well, the corporal won, but the others had their say also, and those Germans will never return to the Fatherland. On another occasion, a man with a bullet-hole through his hand, and part of his leg blown away, was for hours playing "Nap" (a card game), on the top of a Red Cross motor lorry, which was conveying them to the hospital.'

Meanwhile the rest of the borough was reeling from the terrible news of their fallen sons. Brigadier-General Copley and Mrs Bewicke-Copley of Sprotbrough Hall lost their son-in-law, Major Hubert Francis Fitzwilliam Brabazon Foljambe of the King's Royal Rifles amidst a whole raft of Doncaster names that had either fallen on foreign soil or were being held by the Germans as prisoners of war. The support from the townsfolk was outstanding as everyone rallied to generate new ways of supporting the war effort. Boddy's Wool Shop, of 60 and 68 St Sepulchre Gate, and 8 Market Place, told the town's women, 'Our wools are most suitable for knitting socks, helmets, mufflers, belts, etc. for our soldiers, being soft, warm and durable.' The Electra Cinema showed relevant pictures to stir up the emotions of the town starting with, during the first week of September 1914, *Ready, Aye Ready*, a naval film showing the British Fleet in action.

Lord Halifax, of Hickleton Hall, sent letters out to all the colliery managers in his immediate neighbourhood containing the words:

'I shall be ready, within the next few days, to give a lecture in any colliery village in the neighbourhood detailing the circumstances that have led to the war and the efforts that have been made by the Government to preserve the peace of Europe,

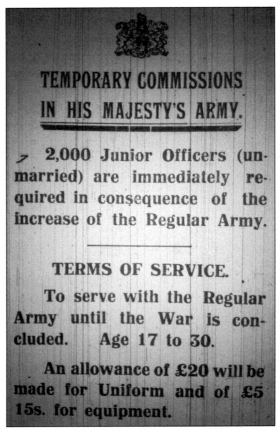

Call for recruits - Doncaster Gazette, August 1914.

based upon the State papers laid before Parliament. I would endeavour in such a lecture to explain the position of our Armies, and to point out the urgent duty that is laid upon everyone, from the highest to the lowest, at the present moment, to do his utmost to reinforce our soldiers in the field, to vindicate the honour of this country, and defend the security of our homes. Any communications addressed to me on the subject will be attended to at once.'

One Doncaster resident, a Mr Harold Begbie, appealed to his
Doncastrians to enlist in the armies by way of a poem entitled *Fo... in*,
which was published in the *Doncaster Chronicle* during October 1914:

*What will you lack sonny, what will you lack, when the girls
line up the street? Shouting their love to the lads, come back,
from the foe they rushed to beat.*

*Will you send a strangled cheer in the sky, and grin 'til your
cheeks are red? But what will you lack when your mate goes
by with a girl who cuts you dead?*

*Where will you look sonny, where will you look, when your
children yet to be, clamour to learn of the part you took in the
war that kept men free?*

*Will you say it was nought to you if France stood up to her foe
or bunked? But where will you look when they give the glance
that tells you they know you flunked?*

*How will you fare sonny, how will you fare, in the far off
winter's night, when you sit by the fire in an old man's chair,
and your neighbours talk of the fight?*

*Will you slink away as it were from a blow, your old head
shamed and bent, or say - "I was not with the first to go, but I
went, thank God, I went."*

*Why do they call sonny, why do they call, for men who are
brave and strong? Is it nought to you if your Country falls, and
right is smashed by wrong?*

*Is it football still and the picture show, the pub and the betting
odds, when your brother's stand to the tyrant's blow and
England's call is God's?*

Mr W.H. Marshall, a reporter working for the *Doncaster Chronicle*,
enlisted shortly after this went to print. Was his conscience pricked, I
wonder?

War funds were cropping up all over town to raise money for the troops and their much needed supplies. Fishlake, near Thorne, opened a war fund at the Endowed School to raise money for the making of socks, sleeping helmets, surgical shirts, cholera belts, and handkerchiefs for the soldiers. Tuby and Sons, the long running Doncaster based show-family, held a 'Grand Organ Recital' of sacred music on 6 September 1914 in the Market Place, in aid of the local relief fund. At Blythe, near Bawtry, the young girls at the vicarage sewing club were busy making covering splints and bandages, while the Sunday collection plate at Owston Ferry church raised £4 13s 9d for the fund. Forty ladies met at Hatfield Victoria Hall to knit and sew for the soldiers and also raised a mammoth £20, and Rossington colliery workers agreed to have 6d per week stopped from their wage in order to help those families whose husbands had been called to the colours. Local businesses were trying desperately, not only to keep their own heads above water at this difficult time, but also the country as a whole with Goodlys Doncaster Furnishing Company, of Station Road, Doncaster, releasing the following advert:

'WAR AND BRITISH INDUSTRY
'Being wishful to find employment, as far as possible, for our employees, and having very large stocks, we have decided to sell any single article, for the time being, at practically cost price to cash purchasers. Every article sold will help on British Industry and will be of benefit to the Country generally, as the circulation of money at the present time is the surest way of preventing depression and unemployment.'

They were joined by others too like Bell Bros Jewellers of 16 and 18 St Sepulchre Gate, Doncaster, who released the following message:

'BUSINESS AND THE WAR
Business has never occupied such an important position as it does today. Business is the mainstay of life. Wars may come and disarrange the order of transaction, but Business will win - must win.'

And Sheard Binnington & Co of 44 High Street, Doncaster, reminds the townsfolk:

'THE TROOPS NEED BLANKETS AND THE NEED IS URGENT - Will you kindly let us know when to call and our van will be there to collect them.'

The people of Doncaster, whether out of obligation, civic pride, or some other reason, felt the need to make use of every resource, financial or otherwise, to ensure the men kept fighting. If it could be done, it was done, and all in the name of the war fund!

Meanwhile in Europe, as the British Army retreated from the onslaught of the German offensive, the French tried desperately to hold on to their lines fearing the worst as the German First Army gained ground and made for Paris. It was France's turn to fight as the British Army hurried south to regroup at the Marne. The German plan was transparent, so much so that we were able to outflank them and send them north to the Chemin des Dames ridge. What a wonderful contrast to those first few days of British involvement as we were finally able to show the German invaders what we were made of which went a long way to restoring our morale.

The summer of 1914 was fading into autumn as the battles continued to rage. The enemy was becoming ever more desperate to reach the French capital and the French and British equally determined to stop them. The by-product of this mirrored determination resulted in the fight moving in a north-westerly direction towards the sea. Each army sidestepped the other towards the French-Belgian coast and the Channel ports of Calais, Dunkirk, Ostend and Zeebrugge. This series of battles became known as 'The Race for the Sea'. What happened next was the beginning of what the First World War has become most famous for – trench warfare.

It was becoming more and more evident that, at this stage at least, we were equally matched so that although no real progress was being made on the part of the German foe we were only successful at holding our own. It was deadlock. Where there was no advancement to be made for either army, the least we could do was to claim the ground that they stood on and refuse to cede. And so they did. Both sides 'dug in', quite literally, and quickly commenced to fortify their side of an erected wire defence using any means possible and any materials they could lay their hands on. By the finish the trenches stretched a colossal 450 miles from the Swiss border to the Belgian coast!

Contrary to popular belief the obligations of the Territorial Army were strictly circumscribed, and it was not in the contract of the men serving in it, unless they specifically accepted such duty, to serve abroad. After mobilisation all ranks were invited to serve abroad. At the outbreak of the war it was not a foregone conclusion that a recruit would be needed in Europe, for many men were required to remain on British soil to guard our coastlines from German invasion. Where the KOYLI were recalled from their training camps in North Yorkshire they were quickly replaced by the Queen's Own Yorkshire Dragoons who, during the early part of 1915, were in training at Scarborough. Although this served the purpose of getting the men into the war mindset, it is questionable whether the instruction stood them in good stead in the field. A local man from middle-gentry parents, Edward Frederick Lindley Wood, 1st Earl of Halifax, of Hickleton Hall, enlisted into the Queen's Own Yorkshire Dragoons. He affectionately refers to his mounted regiment as the 'Cavalry Club'.

He talks of the training he received in Scarborough and how it related to the real-life events that he witnessed in France:

'We were gradually driven to admit that the days of charges on galloping horses with drawn swords, practised by us in the early days on the sands at Scarborough, were unlikely to recur. So we continued, performing various disagreeable tasks, spending much time and energy keeping horses fit that nobody wanted, and eventually exchanging the horse for a faster moving and less time-wasting bicycle. At Scarborough we remained through a long and disagreeable winter, listening on the cliffs at night for sounds that would indicate approaching Germans, and watching the dawn every morning across the grey North Sea.'

Lord Halifax quickly became a major in the Queen's Own and so saw little or nothing of front-line fighting, nevertheless he went which was more than could be said of other men of consequence from the area. He was pleased to finally get to France in July 1915 with the rest of his regiment, for he remarks 'there was a sense of novelty and adventure which was refreshing after months of routine in England'.

And so, eleven months since Doncaster waved its soldiers goodbye at the train stations and barracks, the townspeople were approaching the first anniversary of their leaving. What sort of Christmas would it be for those at home? More importantly what sort of Christmas were our lads to have hundreds of miles from home in the trenches? In fact, the men made of Christmas what they could under the circumstances as Corporal W. Hunt, of the Sherwood Forresters, writing to a Hickleton Main Colliery official, says:

'We had a short Communion service on Christmas Day, and a football match in the afternoon, quite a novelty, just behind the trenches. We returned to the trenches on Boxing Day night with the Germans moving about frequently outside theirs. They keep waving to us and we have done the same to them. I have heard them have singing parades every morning and there has been very little sniping here this Christmas. One would think we were on friendly terms, but I expect we shall have a burst out before very long.'

A second letter from Private George Parr of the York and Lancaster Regiment was sent to his parents in Balby to thank them for the parcels that he received at Christmas time. He writes:

'When you send me another parcel, please send me a few candles and two tins of condensed milk, the candles are to provide us with a light in the trenches at night. Our trenches are only about 300 yards from those of the Germans. We are all happy in spite of the awful weather we are having. We sing at night when there is no firing and the officers join in with us, it would do you good to hear us. I have received the King and Queen's Christmas card and Princess Mary's Christmas box with a photo of herself, which I am sending home and I hope you will get framed for me. I wish I could thank them for the nice presents they sent us.'

And yet another letter came directly to the *Doncaster Gazette* offices from a Doncaster soldier, Driver W. Hartshorn, of the 8th Cavalry Brigade Field Ambulance, on active service in France:

'I should just like to have a few lines put in your paper referring to the soldiers' Christmas in France. Some of us made it up to have an English dinner, as near as possible, viz., roast beef, potatoes and cabbage, followed by sweets and custard. We sang grace in the usual way, and after dinner (which by the way was up to expectations) a toast was proposed, wishing their Majesties the King and Queen a Happy Christmas, and success to the Allied Forces. The toast was translated into French for the benefit of the host and hostess and drunk heartily. The National Anthem was then sung and the *Marseillaise* was hummed by us and sung by the French people. We then had the usual "sing-song" - all the old hymns, and I can assure you that we had a really good time, considering how close to the firing line we are. I ought to have mentioned that we had the dinner at the farm where we were billeted. We also received Princess Mary's Christmas present, consisting of a packet of twenty cigarettes, a packet of tobacco, a pipe and a lovely metal box, along with her photograph and a photograph of their Majesties the King and Queen and a Christmas card with an appropriate greeting.'

It seems that the men, although so very far away from everything that they held dear, did what they could to enjoy Christmas in the most civilised way possible.

CHAPTER 3

The War Rages On

As the Great War continued the by-product, as it always is, was wounds and death, while the lucky ones were being held by the Germans as prisoners of war. Private Thomas Edward Allcock, of 2nd KOYLI, was living a tolerable existence as a prisoner of war in Germany. Employed at the Wire Works in Balby, Allcock like many had to rejoin his old regiment at the outbreak of the war. For more than two months his wife and children had waited in suspense for news of him and then came the information that he had been captured by the Germans in the Mons retreat. He was being held at St Liga prisoners' camp, Paderborn, Germany, and though he was not exactly living on the fat of the land, he was in good health and spirits, and had received the various parcels of luxuries his wife had sent to him. Private Allcock's home was at 1, Chapel Yard, East Laith Gate.

The majority of the men were not so lucky. Private H. Lunn of the 5th Battalion Doncaster Territorials was reported killed, and Sergeant J. R. Worrall, Private F. Depledge, and Private J. Holland of the same battalion were wounded. Mr and Mrs Hemingway and family, of 69 Victoria Street, Doncaster, publicly thanked their friends, 'for the sympathy shown to them on the death of their son, Private H.S. Hemingway of the 1/5th KOYLI, who was killed in France while doing his duty'. Private William Albert Pike of the Doncaster Territorials (KOYLI), and formerly of 10 Beechfield Road, Doncaster, was killed in action on the French Flanders battlefield. He had held a position with the firm of Messrs W. Baddiley and Co, solicitors, of Priory Place. The list goes on... .

Sometimes the news of the deaths was not conveyed quickly and was preceded by a 'missing in action' report. Sometimes the heart-rending news took months to filter through the system. In the case of Private J. Brooks, of C Company (Doncaster Territorials), 1/5th KOYLI, it took five months for the sad news to arrive. Just a few weeks before Brooks' demise he had written a letter to the Mayoress of Doncaster, Mrs Balmforth, which makes the news of his death all the more heartbreaking, for he had hoped, as his fellow comrades had, that they would return to Doncaster unscathed. The letter reads:

'Dear Madam,
'Just a line to say that we of the 1/5th KOYLI somewhere in France, are very interested to hear of your support for us. The people of Doncaster do not realise the horror of grim war and death quite the same as the lads who left the town on that fateful day last August. You will doubtless be pleased to know that we Doncaster lads follow with deep interest the 'doings' of the ancient and historic town of 'Donny', and we are much delighted by the report of the recent recruiting campaign in your midst. We have just come out of the trenches for six days and are having a well-earned rest which we deeply appreciate. We can only add that the thought of the old town is ever with us, and that when in the trenches our topic is 'shall we see the Leger this year?' - I remain, Yours Sincerely, Pte J. Brooks.'

Each day the town received news of yet more fallen soldiers and both the *Doncaster Chronicle* and the *Doncaster Gazette* were crammed full of such bad news. The editors tried in vain to balance out the misery by featuring regular articles on the enemy's misfortunes on the battlefield, though this was little or no comfort to those families who had lost loved ones.

In a January issue of the *Doncaster Gazette* a mother's pride in the knowledge that four of her sons had, and were, fighting the fine fight abroad was featured. Mrs Clarson of 25 Washington Grove, Bentley, told how one of her sons, William Henry Clarson, had already met his end in the trenches of France and another was now at the Front fighting for his life. Two other sons were in training in England waiting for their inevitable mobilisation, and she had already lost her eldest son in the

The Clarson Brothers - Clockwise from top left, Albert 18, Nathan 23, William Henry 27, George 24.

African Wars at the beginning of the century. William Henry, aged 27, was working at Bullcroft Colliery at the outbreak of the war at which point he was recalled to his old regiment, the Sherwood Foresters. He was killed in action on the Aisne on 20 October 1914; his brother George, aged 24, was now representing the family at the Front. George had taken part in the whole campaign from Mons to Marne, Aisne to Flanders, and had received shell wounds which had incapacitated him for a while. Eager to return to his comrades however, he made a quick recovery before returning to his regiment. Nathan, aged 23, and Albert, aged 18, Mrs Clarson's other sons, were wearing their army uniforms with pride in England whilst training, having left secure and well-paid employment in the Bullcroft and Bentley Collieries. Mrs Clarson had one more son who was too young to enlist and who did an excellent job of looking after the house and his mother while his elder siblings were away.

The contrasting article that would have offered little compensation for Mrs Clarson read:

'A Copenhagen telegram says the last German casualty lists which have been received give the losses up to the beginning of December, 1914. These are the 115th Prussian, 129th Bavarian, 84th Württemberg, and the 82nd Saxon lists. The Prussian losses alone amount to about one million men. If the losses comprised in other German casualty lists are included and those for December are added, the total will reach about two million men.'

Despite the losses, men and boys continued to flock to the recruiting stations with 147 more recruits enlisting in January 1915. These included 115 former pupils from Morley Place School in Conisborough and over 700 men who had been in the employ of the Yorkshire Main Colliery Company at Edlington. With the fierce fighting on the Continent came the need for medical care both in France and in England. A good number of temporary hospitals sprang up across the borough erected inside large halls and country houses. The Mansion House was prepared for the possible eventuality of its being needed as a hospital and medical equipment was delivered and stored there, the Corporation having earlier made the decision 'to give the Mayor discretionary power with regards to the use of the said Mansion House for military purposes in case of urgency'.

In addition the staff at the Doncaster VAD (Voluntary Aid Detachment) continued to be fully employed at the Arnold Auxiliary Hospital:

'Six convalescent soldiers left on Monday morning for light duties back with their battalions abroad, but a dozen fresh cases came in from Sheffield in the afternoon, and there are now 25 patients – the full complement provided for in the Thorne Road institution. Those who so kindly and regularly support the hospital through gifts of various kinds will be encouraged to

The Arnold Hospital, fundraising event.

continue this welcome help when they learn that the discharged convalescents speak in the most enthusiastic terms of the kindness they have received in "Edenfield", both from the VAD staff and from the many kind friends who contribute to make the time pass pleasantly for them.'

The latest arrivals at Edenfield were from the Base Hospital at Sheffield but they were not all recovering from wounds, although some of them had been pretty severely mauled by shrapnel. The trouble with some of the soldiers was frostbite which was likely to be equally as disabling as the wounds from shot or shell and may have been quite as serious in its permanent results, as a number of men had had to undergo an amputation of the affected member. The *Gazette* reads:

'In this connection, very curious was the experience of one of these convalescents, a sergeant in the Dorset Regiment. He was on the scene in Belgium in the earliest stages of the war, took part in the historic retreat from Mons, and has fought in many a

Loversall Hall Military Hospital 1915.

fierce engagement since. For three months he was out there and never received a scratch at the hands of the enemy – but the bitter enemy in the water-logged trenches marked him down at last, and sent him home with both legs severely frostbitten. "You don't know you've got it at first," he said, "You simply think your legs are very cold, and that when you get out of the trench you will be able to march it off. Your legs and feet are stiffened and numbed and it's like walking on a pair of stilts. I know that when I came out of the trench for the last time I was able to hobble along on the soft ground, but as soon as I got on the hard ground it was like my feet weighed several pounds each. But the worst part of frostbite is the recovery – when they have got your legs packed up with dressings and wool, and the circulation is coming back. It's like chronic pins and needles and you can't get any sleep at night for it. Afterwards, the feet are so sensitive that anyone walking across the floor close to you sends a nasty tingling pain up your leg. The worst part of the campaign was the weather, the cold and the rain flooding the trenches."'

He gratefully acknowledged the ample way in which the trenches were supplied with food and clothing, both by the army authorities and the numerous voluntary agencies at home. One of the worst parts of the bad weather was the way that the rain and the mud got into the working parts of the men's rifles causing the bolts to jam, so hindering the extraction of the used cartridges in readiness for the firing of the next one.

Archdeacon Sandford of St George's Parish Church, Doncaster, offered words of encouragement to the people of Doncaster with perhaps a subliminal message to those who had not yet fully committed to the cause. He says:

'I wish you all a Happy New Year, and by that I mean that I hope we shall all of us rise to our opportunities this New Year, and each of us play the man, and give unstintingly of our best for the common need, and see this great war successfully concluded as a result of our sacrifices in a great and good cause. This is no time to think of happiness, except so far as it lies directly in the path of duty. The Empire has a duty to perform, probably the greatest and heaviest it has ever yet undertaken, and each one of us has a duty, and a hard and costly duty, too, to the Empire, and we must see to it that it is done, and well done, and then a deep and lasting happiness will result from it, and not otherwise.'

On another occasion he makes a statement unlikely to fill the mothers of the town with confidence of their sons' safe return. In his monthly letter to the parishioners Sandford talks of the 5th Battalion KOYLI saying that they had done so well already and given a good account of themselves in the field. He continues by saying that if any of those serving abroad or those about to go should unfortunately fall on the field of honour in defence of their country, he should very much like to arrange for a memorial service in each case. He concludes: 'We admire them in life; we will honour them in death.'

Fund raising was still very much in evidence as the townspeople rallied to raise more and more money for the troops. According to official figures it was costing the country 1.5 million pounds per day to keep our men fighting and the Kaiser at bay; never had there been a more pressing need for financial support than during the Great War. Grahame's Military Band of 45 performers played a concert in the Corn Exchange, Doncaster, assisted by members of the 5th, 6th and 7th West Riding Regiments of the Royal Army Medical Corps, to raise much needed money for the clothing fund of the 5th Battalion KOYLI. Many military officers were in attendance along with Aldermen and other members of the Corporation:

'From a musical point of view the concert was distinctly creditable, conducted as they were by a musician of the calibre of Mr W.E. Glen, late of the Grenadier Guards' Band. A notable selection in the programme was "The Battle of Mons",

Canon Sandford, Vicar of Doncaster.

especially composed by Mr Glen. It was enthusiastically received. This was the third series of concerts organised by Mrs. Grahame, who since November has handed over to war funds £20 11s 4d.'

Money was also being raised for the Belgian Relief Fund to the tune of £849 12s 9d the breakdown of which was: Mr G. Fogg, proceeds of sale of West Highland Terrier £11 1s; proceeds of concert at Highfield Road Primitive Methodist Church, £11; Miss Shearman, £3 4s 6d; Mrs. Blumhardt, proceeds of tea at Wadworth, £2 6s; Blaxton Wesleyan Chapel, £2 3s; Mr Roberts, £2; Corporation Gas Works, £1 19s. 6d; Morley Road Methodist Church, £1 7s 6d; Messrs. T.W. Cawood and Son, £1; Messrs. Woodhouse and Co. brass finishers, 14s.

One evening the Doncaster Tradesman's Association entertained about 1,000 of the troops that were stationed in the Doncaster district at the Corn Exchange. The troops present included men of the RAMC, ASC, RFA, RE, and the 5th and 9th Durham Light Infantry. Also in attendance was the Retford Concert Party, including Mrs Scaife, Miss L. Pacey, Messrs Harry Scaife, Reginald Harrison and Frank Wheeldon. Entertainment was courtesy of the Brothers St John, musical comedians and dancers from the Palace Theatre, by kind permission of Mr North, Chester and Dottridge. Light refreshments were served during the evening and the men appeared to thoroughly enjoy themselves. Colonel Gunner voiced his appreciation in a vote of thanks to the Tradesman's Association, which Captain Walkely seconded. In response, the Mayor, Councillor S. Balmforth expressed the pleasure it gave the tradesmen to entertain the troops in the district. A great deal of money was raised for the war fund.

Meanwhile, at Armthorpe, even the children were getting involved in the cause. The pupils of Armthorpe School gave a concert in the school house which raised £4 16s 6d. It consisted of a series of songs and dances in character. The concert included performances like 'Babes in the Wood', 'Dolly Town', 'Fairy Land', 'Quack Doctor', and a sketch entitled Britannia and her Allies. The rector presided and at the conclusion congratulated Miss Smith, the headmistress, and all the staff 'for the excellence of the entertainment provided through their labours, which must have been very arduous to procure the results achieved'.

KOYLI band on parade.

The object of the concert was to raise money to create a parcel which was sent to France for 'our boys'. Each parcel contained cake, cigarettes, fruit, sweets, and a short greeting from the teachers and staff of the Armthorpe School. The parcels were dispatched to each of the sixteen boys who were serving at the Front and who were living in Armthorpe when they joined the colours. Shortly afterwards a grateful reply came back home from France, 'Our sincere thanks for the delightful little Christmas parcels which we have all received. The articles could not possibly have been more aptly chosen, and they were thoroughly appreciated by every one of us.'

Mrs Pickering, representing the Doncaster Voluntary Aid Detachment, stated that the Stores Depot of the VAD had been transferred from the Mansion House to number 19 Hall Gate. From this depot more than 3,100 garments had been dispatched for use at the Front. The stock was now reduced to 300 articles and more gifts of clothing, shirts, socks, scarves and under-garments were very urgently needed. Most of the townsfolk were managing to empty their purses for the various funds, all except one it seems, as listed under 'Miscellaneous Wants' in the *Doncaster Gazette*, July 1915, appears this advert:

'WANTED - Good home for Baby Boy; three months old; must be respectable; will pay weekly sum. - Write, Box 361, Doncaster Gazette Office.'

There was a special notice sent out for the attention of local farmers, 'PRESERVE OUR FLOCKS AND HERDS TO MAINTAIN OUR MEAT SUPPLY'. The Board of Agriculture and Fisheries was urging all farmers to raise as much stock as possible during the war. Advice included not sending breeding and immature stock to the butcher simply because the prices were attractive now; not killing calves but rearing them, and not to reduce stock. 'WHEN YOU CANNOT BUY STORES, BUY CALVES.' They made the recommendations not only for the national welfare, but because they believed them to be for the ultimate benefit of British agriculture.

It was becoming obvious to all concerned that the war was not going to be over quickly. There was a great deal of forward planning and no-one was exempt from service, for the need for all manner of skills was urgent in these austere times. While the 'bread-winners' were away factories, coal mines and railway works needed to be manned – or 'womanned'. Nurses were needed for the many temporary hospitals and an amusing story comes from the father of one such nurse, told to a group in Doncaster:

'I was visiting the hospital the other day, and had sat down by the bedside of a Lancashire miner, who had been very badly wounded, and talked to him of the war. By and by my daughter came into the room, and I said, "I hope my daughter is looking after you all right." He broke into a loud smile, winked his eye heavily at me, and said, "She's a treat".'

The local girls tending the sick and wounded soldiers, must have been a welcome sight for the men who were miles from home. Some of the temporary hospitals even had miraculous effects it seemed, as a story of the time relates. Private Joseph McDonald, of the Highland Light Infantry, whose home was in Glasgow, recovered his speech at the Arnold Auxiliary Military Hospital, Thorne Road, Doncaster, in a remarkable manner. The soldier lost his speech six months previously through shell-shock. He was enjoying the Christmas festivities with other wounded soldiers when, in the excitement 'produced by fun and frolic', he suddenly discovered that his speech had returned.

Casualties did not always come from the Front however, for on 21 February 1916, Private Thomas Allen of the 7th Nottinghamshire and Derby Supernumerary Corps was killed whilst on guard at the Sandall Bridge over the Great Central Railway, near Doncaster. On leaving the guard's shelter on the side of the line, Allen was caught by a passing train and 'cut to pieces'. This was the third fatality of its kind which had occurred at the same spot during the time that the bridge had been guarded.

Another death that shocked and saddened the town, although not connected with the war, was that of Alfred Roe, aged 50. Alfred was a miner living at Woodlands Model Village, near Doncaster. He was cycling in Doncaster on a Saturday when the streets were very greasy through rain. At the junction of St Sepulchre Gate and Printing Office Street, his cycle skidded and he was thrown under the hooves of two heavy horses attached to a brewery dray. One of the animals trampled on him. A policeman seized the horses' heads while a man dragged Roe from under their feet, very badly injured. 'He was taken with all speed to the Doncaster Royal Infirmary' where he later died from his injuries.

As another year reached its climax at Christmas 1916 an impressive memorial service was held at St Mary's Church, Wheatley to honour the fallen. A special invitation was sent out by the Vicar, the Rev. E.P. Cook, to the relatives of all the fallen heroes known to him and seats were reserved at the front of the nave. After the second lesson, a number of Boy Scouts accompanied the Vicar from the choir stalls to the chancel steps, one of them carrying a Union Jack draped in black. The flag-bearer remained beside the Vicar during the reading of the service. The Vicar then preached from St John's Gospel, on the text 'Greater love hath no man than this. That a man lay down his life for his friends.' Speaking of those from the parish who had laid down their own lives in Belgium, France, Gallipoli, Mesopotamia, on the sea, or in the hospitals of the homeland, he said that we honoured and respected their memories and that their names would be handed down to future generations with affectionate esteem.

He then read out a list of those parishioners of Wheatley known to have died in the service of their country.

Interior of St Mary's Church, Wheatley ©Kenneth Paver 2011.

Sailors: Joshua Bell, C. Brooks, George Seaman, W. A. Newborn.
Soldiers: Silas Black, William Burgess, Frank Cook, William Colley, Edward Coulthard, Herbert Dalton, J. Earnshaw, James Percival Geeson, Charles William Harsley, Harry Innocent, Thomas Alfred Leggott, Arthur S. Lanfear, Arthur Markham, H. H. Perrett, Joseph Parkin, Walter Richardson, James Edward Sigston, Bert Sutton, Ernest Tate, Harry Axup, Tom Foster.
Airman: R. E. Scott, Petty Officer of the Royal Navy Air Force.

The congregation was so large that it could not be contained inside the building. It seemed that the whole community had attended to offer their condolences and to demonstrate their support for the bereaved.

Doncaster was at the centre of the fight when it came to air power, having a permanent aerodrome constructed by the Government for the Royal Flying Corps (RFC). The three large 'Belfast' hangars, each measuring a colossal 200ft by 64ft, were sited to the north of the racecourse on the opposite side of Leger Way, taking up a large proportion of what is now the Westminster Crescent estate of Intake. The original intention for the aerodrome was for training purposes only as the perceived threat of an invasion from the air was not entertained. Not, that is, until the second and third years of the Great War. German aircraft called Gothas crossed the sea in 1916 to bomb England, particularly the south. The Zeppelin threat was also very real and we eventually came to recognise it and began to prepare for the eventuality that this town might become a target.

The Doncaster aerodrome came under the command of 6 Brigade, North-East Area, 24 Group, 46th Wing for Home Defence, and 16 Group, 8th Wing for Training. The first units that came to Doncaster for training arrived on 1 January 1916 in the forms of the 15 RAS (Reserve Aeroplane Squadron), and 15 RS (Reserve Squadron). They had various aircraft at their disposal including H. Farmans, Avro 504s and BE2Cs and had the backing of the War Office who had, in 1915, after the Kaiser's introduction of the deadly airborne weaponry, instructed that the station be created at Doncaster. Immediately before and during its construction in 1915, a small fighter detachment had been based on the racecourse itself but had left before the RFC station was opened.

The new base welcomed its first detachment, 41 Squadron equipped with BE2Cs, later to be replaced by 33 Squadron from Bramham Moor. The first real excitement for the lads stationed at the Doncaster aerodrome came on the night of 4 April 1916 when two Zeppelins, en route to London, were blown off course and found themselves at the north Yorkshire coast. Captain A.A.B. Thomson of 15 RAS took off at 2300 hours from Doncaster in a BE2C to intercept them. After a lengthy search he failed to see the enemy and crashed at Tealby, near Market Rasen, at 0145 hours. Another interception was scrambled on the night of 2 May 1916 when more than a dozen Zeppelins were crossing the coast to England. One of the BE2Cs was sent but, again, the attempt was unsuccessful. It would be November 1916 before a successful flying mission would present itself.

Flying in those days was a dangerous business. On one occasion, an Avro 504 crashed and caught fire with the pilot trapped inside, the bystanders being utterly helpless. Shortly afterwards, within minutes in fact, another Avro 504 crashed on Leger Way between the airfield

Avro 504K by B. Robertson.

and the racecourse. The accidents and incidents in connection with the Doncaster aerodrome are too numerous to mention here. Some of the dead were buried at the Hyde Park cemetery in Doncaster. But, as if we weren't losing enough of our lads, the following advertisement appeared in the *Doncaster Chronicle* newspaper in September 1917:

'A CHANCE FOR ADVENTUROUS BOYS - A thousand more boys are required for the Royal Flying Corps. Those with knowledge or an aptitude for engineering or woodwork are the most urgently needed, and teachers of these subjects at technical schools would do well to keep an eye on suitable pupils who have these acquirements. The following are some of the conditions:- Medical Classification "A"; Age - 16 to 17½; Period of Service - duration of war; Education - must have passed standard VI; Pay - from 8d to 2s per day. Enrolment is at the recruiting office, Trafford Street.'

To my knowledge only one account of life at the aerodrome survives, coming from Lieutenant W.M. Fry, as he wrote about his stay in Doncaster in 1916 before the station was fully completed:

'I arrived at number 15 RS at the end of May after six weeks of elementary training with others of my course for advanced flying training. The Commander was Captain J.E.A. Baldwin of the 8th Hussars, later Air Marshal. The Sergeants' Mess and other offices were housed in the racecourse buildings and the Officers' Mess was in what is now the Grand St Leger Hotel. The hotel, then just a large house, had been used in peacetime by Lord Lonsdale for Leger Week. The aircraft were Avros, Armstrong Whitworths, and a few BE2Cs. A number of the instructors were highly decorated officers on rest from France. The advanced training started on Avros followed by going solo on Armstrong Whitworths.

RFC Depot Doncaster covering most of what is now Westminster Crescent.

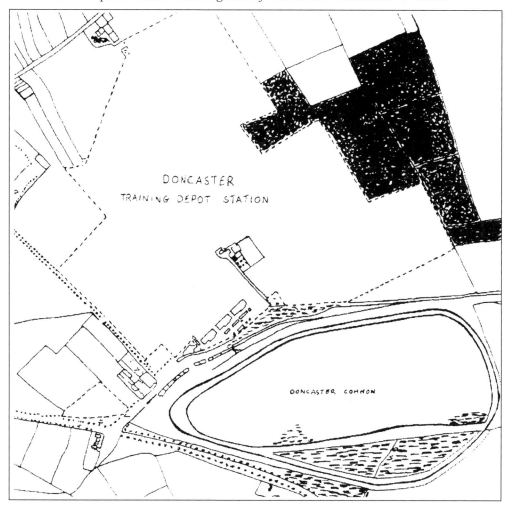

'Much of the training consisted of cross-country flying together with ground lectures. The students could choose where they wanted to fly but the exercise had to include at least two landings at other aerodromes. Their course had to be approved by their Flight Commander and the aircraft had to be signed off as 'fit for the flight'. One of the most popular trips was to the old racecourse at Scarborough calling in at York, Catterick, and Bramham Moor on the way back. The airfield at Scarborough was run by the Royal Navy and was little more than a mile from the town. The Navy lads happily laid on transport for us, usually in the form of a Rolls-Royce, and conveyed us into Scarborough where we would have lunch in a hotel on the sea front before returning home. We had little faith in our compasses and usually navigated our way by following the railway lines as most of them in the area led to Doncaster.

'The people of Doncaster came in large numbers to see the flying, although we suspected that what they really wanted to see was the crashes. Some weekends, when there were more spectators, some of the pilots would take a dummy up with them and throw it out of the plane from a great height, the ambulance men would then rush out with a stretcher to collect the fake body much to everyone's excitement. We were paid 8 shillings per day which was a very handsome wage for the time, although it was more like danger money as the life expectancy at the Front in France was only a matter of weeks. When we had accumulated a specified number of flying hours and had reached the required standard we were awarded our wings. There was no formal 'wings' parade, it was just the Commanding Officer announcing in the mess that certain pilots had passed and that was it. The following morning the pilots would appear in the mess with their new wings. Then they were granted a few days leave before they left for France.'

The Royal Flying Corps was reincarnated as the Royal Air Force (RAF) in April 1918.

It was not just the training of pilots that Doncaster was famous for as we also had a fine reputation for the manufacture of aeroplanes. Any production and manufacturing company that had the relevant skills could adapt their machinery to produce aircraft. Such was the demand for more and more aircraft that Pegler's of Doncaster were awarded a contract to produce fifty Sopwith Cuckoo torpedo carriers, although this amount was optimistic. The required number was eventually reduced to twenty, the remaining thirty being taken by another firm in Hull. By the end of the war, only one of the planes had been produced and it took until the end of 1919 to produce five in total!

By 1919 the aerodrome was no longer required and was closed, the hangars taken down and re-erected on a new industrial estate being constructed on the road between Blaxton and Finningley. Originally, Earl Fitzwilliam, who had an interest in the Sheffield car firm, Simplex, planned to use the Doncaster aerodrome for car assembly and storage but this plan was never realised. One of the hangars, however, was left in situ and was used as a bus garage until the 1970s. The hangar was demolished to make way for an expansion of the Doncaster bus garaging and storage facility.

Meanwhile, during 1916, Doncaster men were recuperating in temporary hospital beds set up at hundreds of sites across the kingdom suffering from injuries received at the hands of the enemy. In Chelsea, Sergeant William Micklethwaite, a Doncaster Royal Engineer, was having his eye removed as a result of an explosion at the Front. Micklethwaite, of Elsworth Street, was a brass finisher at the Doncaster Plant Works before the outbreak of the war and had previously served with the Doncaster Volunteers before 1914. Another Doncaster Royal Engineer, Sapper Herbert Cary, of Carr View Avenue, was in the Wharncliffe Hospital at Sheffield recovering from the effects of shell-shock and a dose of German gas. He was cycling at the Front when a shell fell and knocked him unconscious.

Lucky escapes were not uncommon too as the following stories from the *Gazette* show:

'WHEATLEY SOLDIER WOUNDED - Private A. J. Drury, Yorkshire Regiment, younger son of Mr and Mrs George Drury of 34 St. Mary's Road, Doncaster, was wounded in the recent fighting and is now in a London hospital. He was struck by shrapnel shot which passed through the arm and struck against a cigarette case in his breast pocket. But for this obstacle it would have entered the body with possibly fatal results. His Colonel and other officers of the Battalion were all killed in the same action. Private Drury, known to his friends as 'Bert', was formerly in the business carried out by his father and uncle in St Sepulchre Gate. He joined the army in the first months of the war whilst on holiday at Scarborough and has been at the Front since April 1915.'

'Private Horace Scholes, a member of the KOYLI, and of 89 Christ Church Road, Doncaster, lay in hospital at Birmingham suffering from shrapnel wounds in the back. He was knocked over during an attack on a wood and had to crawl on his hands and knees for about four miles before reaching a British dressing station. On the way he passed two dressing stations belonging to our Allies where he was urged to come in and receive medical attention, but he preferred to push on to his own lines. He accepted a cup of coffee from the Allied ambulance men, however, and acknowledges very gratefully the kindness he received at their hands. He had come through so far without a scratch although most of his companions had fallen. He had met his brother quite by chance the day before at the Front and they had celebrated the occasion with a wonderful tea of tinned salmon, pineapple chunks and bread and butter.'

Meanwhile, back in Doncaster, all were not behaving as they should have done as the following examples demonstrate. In Bentley a coal miner by the name of George Stuttings was fined six shillings for riding a bicycle without a red rear light. A soldier's wife was in trouble too. Annie E. Mellor was sent to prison for two months after a summons was brought against her by the NSPCC for cruelty to her six children by keeping her house in a 'dirty and verminous condition'. The house was full of vermin and in a generally wretched state. It was ascertained that the defendant drank heavily and on one occasion was seen singing, quarrelling and thrashing one of the boys. She could not say that she couldn't afford to keep a clean home as she was in receipt of thirty-three shillings per week from the Government and had no rent to pay.

Not even demobbed soldiers were squeaky-clean as a Mons hero was charged with theft from a dwelling house. James Walmsley, with the help of his wife Ada, had gained illegal entry into Avenue House and stolen carpets and linoleum to the value of £20. The items were the property of Herbert Ridgill, a builder of Armthorpe Lane. On 23 November 1915, a search was made of the ex-soldier's home at 25 Morley Road, Wheatley where the articles were recovered by Detective Sergeant Dixon. Walmsley was fined £1 but his wife suffered worse, being committed to prison for one month.

Not all news was so dire though. Sergeant J.E. Webster, a Brodsworth miner-soldier, won the Military Medal for an exceedingly valorous deed. Five of the men of Sergeant Webster's company lay wounded and under heavy fire. He was one of the first men to respond to the commanding officer's call for volunteers to fetch in the wounded men. He succeeded in bringing all five wounded men back to the shelter but unfortunately only one of them survived. Webster, who passed through his perilous enterprise unscathed, was serving with the KOYLI, enlisting at the outbreak of the war and attaining the rank of sergeant within a year. Prior to enlistment he worked as a miner at Brodsworth Colliery and lived at 100 The Park, Woodlands.

Another local hero, Sergeant Harry Justice of Church House, Cantley was given an honourable mention in the list of recommendations for gallant and distinguished conduct in the field.

The year 1916 as a whole proved that a town will behave like a town whether there was a war or not. Men continued to lay down their lives for the good of their fellow men and families and whole communities showed their respect and gratitude in every way possible. In every town and city there will always be a core of kind-hearted folk that work tirelessly to help others with inner satisfaction being the one and only motivator and there will always be a minority who spoil things for others. There was one powerful sentiment however that united the townsfolk – that the war's end was long overdue. The war that was supposed to be over by Christmas was now into its third year without any signs of abating. What was 1917 to bring?

CHAPTER 4

A Daily Struggle

The year 1917 began with a real struggle for both the men on the Front and those left behind in Doncaster. The people of Sprotbrough welcomed the New Year by holding a memorial service at St Mary's Church for the Lord of the Manor's eldest son and heir. The requiem was in memory of the late Redvers Lionel Calverley Bewicke-Copley, Coldstream Guards. In attendance were the boy's father, Brigadier-General R.C.A. Bewicke-Copley, KBE CB and Mrs Bewicke-Copley, with workmen, servants on the estate, the tenantry, villagers and others, with sympathies being sent from Mr E. Walker Jackson, Chairman of the Doncaster West Riding Court with the words, 'Major Copley was a Magistrate for this Riding and, had he been spared, would have been a valuable addition to the Bench. If any consolation can be found in this sad circumstance it is in the fact that he gave his life for his King and Country at a most critical time.'

To go so long without a skilled workforce was beginning to take its toll on the town. Many of the men who had left their positions in the factories and mines would never return and so there was a real urgency for temporary to permanent recruits. One such position needing to be filled was that of an apprentice 'trimmer' at the 'Plant' works, Hexthorpe, as Mr and Mrs Bramley of 74 Somerset Road, Hyde Park, received the news of the death in action of their third son, Seaman Jack Bramley RND, which had occurred on 13 November 1916 whilst serving on the Western Front. Elsewhere, Bentley Colliery was facing a similar predicament as Sapper Charlie Fear of the Royal Engineers was killed in action on 10 December 1916. Charlie, a married man and father, lived at 19, Broughton Avenue, Bentley. He was well liked by his colleagues at Bentley Pit. He had previously been wounded and gassed on 15 October 1916 and had appeared on the 'missing in action' list because he had been unconscious at the time of being removed to a hospital and all trace of him was lost by the rest of his company. He recovered quickly and was soon back at the Front only to be killed weeks later. Even more sad was the fact that his brother, who was in the same company of Engineers, had to assist in the burial.

Charlie Fear.

To raise community spirit and to maintain the morale of the injured men the Mayor and Corporation hosted a hospitality evening at the Mansion House for the patients of the local auxiliary war hospitals. The Mayor and Mayoress, Councillor and Mrs George Raithby, welcomed the men to the Mansion House. There were 130 soldiers and 30 nurses in attendance from the Arnold and St George's Hospitals, together with the hospital at Loversall Hall. The men were accompanied by Mrs Pickering, the Commandant of the Arnold hospital, Sister Pease of St George's, and Mrs Skipwith of Loversall Hall, along with members of the executive and nursing staffs. The entertainment was enjoyed by other dignitaries too including Mr R.A.H. Tovey, Town Clerk, the Reverend John Pickup of Sheffield, the Reverend F. Gordon Mee and Councillor Jackson. Everyone arrived via taxi cabs laid on by the Mayor at his own expense. There was an informal musical programme before tea was served in the banqueting rooms where the tables had been 'spread for a knife and fork tea. No detail that could minister to their comfort and enjoyment had been overlooked, and at the end of the meal each man received a packet of cigarettes for consumption during the evening'.

The Mayor expressed the pleasure that it gave the Mayoress and himself to entertain them and said:

'You have fought for your King and Country and for the welfare of your families at home. I hope that those that cannot go to the war themselves will always recognise their great indebtedness to you for the valuable work you have done on their behalf. You have been fighting for liberty and justice and for the continued freedom of your countrymen and we recognise the valour you have shown, the risks you have run, and in your general conduct, that you are true Englishmen fighting in the cause of the right. I believe that right is on your side and that ultimately right will succeed. I believe from the signs of the times that things have looked very black indeed but the horizon is now somewhat brighter and the general outlook is improving. I hope that sooner, rather than later, that peace will be proclaimed and victory will have attended your arms, and that everything possible will be done to prevent future wars.'

The majority of the residents were still doing all they could for the local funds as the *Doncaster Gazette* reveals:

'Benefit Football - A match between the Wire Works Girls and Balby Old School was played on the Rovers' ground, kindly lent, on Saturday morning. About 500 spectators assembled, and victory rested with the girls by 4-1. About £7 5s was realised on behalf of the Local Relief Fund.'

But not everyone was doing their bit for the town. Another feature in the very same edition of the *Gazette* reads:

'Too Much Light - A number of persons were summoned to Doncaster West Riding Court under the Lighting Order, and fines of 15s were imposed on the following: Arthur Young, miner, Askern; Arthur Walker, cowman, Wadworth; William Spencer and James Hackett, miners, New Edlington; Joseph Holmes, miner, Carcroft; William Corby, miner, Rossington; Charles H. Brown, grocer, Carcroft; George Scott, steward, Ashmount Club; Frederick W. Deighton (Messrs Morris, Little, and Co.) Priory Place; Robert Whitley, Travis Row; William Davies, 47 Hexthorpe Road; William Cordingley, Earlesmere Avenue; Albert Simpson, Lister Avenue; Joseph Rafferty, Balby Road; Fred Lambert, Albany Road and Eliza Powell, Alexandra Road.'

Women were called in to keep the factories running as this picture shows.
Female workers at The Plant works.

The town was still struggling with the manufacture of the items that were needed for daily living let alone the production of everything that the soldiers needed. It was not just the manufacturing industries either that were under a great strain as Mother Nature was also interfering with food supplies. The *Western Daily Press* of 17 March 1917 declared:

'FOOD DIFFICULTY - The Shortage of Potatoes
Business at the Doncaster Potato Market, which claims to be the largest in the north of England, was at a standstill on Saturday, and a potato famine in Yorkshire may be said to have commenced. Intending buyers who visited the town from long distances met with no success and had to return home empty-handed.

'At the National Conference of Working Class Associations at Bradford, Mr Orwin said that we were only at the beginning of our difficulties with regard to the food supply. There were excited scenes in the market on the Saturday morning when one farmer had several tons of the vegetable on offer. The selling started at 10 o'clock and continued until 1 o'clock during which time about 1,500 people were served with 4lbs each. There was such a rush for the stand that the borough police had to be called in to regulate the crowd and to settle arguments between the 500 plus individuals who went without.'

Everyone was affected by the austere times, not just the poor. Reports were filtering back to Doncastrians of the effects of the food shortage on the more affluent members of society. Sir Charles Nicholson talked of meal times with his fellow ministers in the House of Commons saying, 'Twenty people including Ministers sat down to their evening meal last night. No butcher's meat was allowed and very few potatoes were given. There was also a shortage of tobacco supplies, hence the term 'fine-cut'.

One local man turned to poaching from a nearby estate to put food on the table. Joseph Laking, a collier living at Highfields, appeared at the Borough Court for a game trespass at Brodsworth. Mr Bowman, the gamekeeper, said that he had seen Laking 'with a snap-dog at the Brodsworth road'. He was examining the fields with a pair of glasses before crossing the field and entering a plantation. He was fined 20 shillings.

Readers could be forgiven for assuming that the 'pound shop' is a modern addition to the High Street but they would be wrong for the 'Empire' – a five and a half penny bazaar, had opened its doors at 59, French Gate. Their slogan, which must have carried an attractive appeal to those desperately trying to make ends meet read, 'Have you noticed how prices are going up regularly week by week? Our prices are still the same! Buy from the Empire Bazaar - nothing above 5½d.'

The fighting men worried about their lack of good weaponry and equipment as they faced the prospect of defending our shores with sub-standard and out-dated guns. Lord French addressed volunteers nearing the end of their training and on the brink of their postings to the Front. He reminded the troops that we had been at war for well over two years and that alone was taking its toll on the country's manufacturing infrastructure. Every sort of manufacture was under a great strain. In addition, we were not only having to supply our own armies, but also

having to help arm those of our Allies. To the relief of the gathered men, Lord French announced that the situation was now a great deal better, and that the Government was now able to do much more in supplying the needs of the Volunteers and placing them in an efficient condition on the field. He also said that any man before him could leave in a fortnight, according to their terms of engagement, but he was sure that if he asked any of them whether they wished to leave during the course of the war they would indignantly deny the suggestion, and think it even an insult.

It was very difficult to gauge the depth of an individual's patriotism until it had been tried in the fire of that stern discipline needed on the Front line. Up to this point, the training of the new infantry soldier recruits focused very much on the use of the rifle, but that was about to change for the supreme importance of the rifle was now powerfully challenged by the machine-gun, the hand and rifle grenade and the bayonet. Brigadier-General Allington Bewick Copley, the County

Commandant of Sprotbrough Hall, was also present to inspect the troops and said, 'It is most encouraging that at this period of the war I should see so fine a body of men before me'. The ceremony was observed by the Lord Mayor of Sheffield, the Master Cutler, the Mayors of Doncaster, Barnsley, Wakefield and Rotherham and Chief Constables of Sheffield, the West Riding, and others.

Lord French summed up his speech by quashing a rumour that the Volunteers were not needed. He brought a message directly from His Majesty the King who had said, 'The great appreciation I have for the Volunteers cannot be uttered in words. I thank you all personally for your loyalty and patriotism to this country. I appreciate my Volunteers as much as any other of my forces and I also know that the Government and War Office consider you a necessary and valuable asset in the problem of home defence. Do not imagine that the possibility of invasion is a fable or a fairy-tale for it is absolutely possible and if it came about, you would have to take up active service just as the men in France are giving active service.'

Major E.F.L. Wood - Lord Halifax.

Separately, Major E.F.L. Wood, formerly of Temple Newsham, latterly of Hickleton Hall, commended the work of that other faithful local squadron, the Queen's Own Yorkshire Dragoons. Major Wood was in command of the squadron that had done great work at the Front since July 1915. There was now a realisation that the Germans were hampered just as much by the internal difficulties in that area of hostilities as we were in the beginning. He remarked on the changing perception of the war in our minds at home. We began in 1914 with epic failures, under-preparations, and under-estimations. We ran from the safety of our lines straight at the Germans expecting them to flee to the hills. They did not. They fought a hard battle and sent us running for our lives. This legacy had prevailed in Doncaster from that point forward. Deep down, wives and mothers expected never to see their loved ones again, they believed the war to be a suicide mission that we were destined to lose. Major Wood sensed that our minds were being made over and that we were now daring to

The Queen's Own Yorkshire Dragoons being inspected by the King at Blendecques, near Calais.

hope of victory. After many an initial trial our armies were suddenly making progress, yes men were still dying by the thousands on a daily basis, but progress was being achieved on a scale that we had not yet experienced. The Royal Navy, that quiet stealthy force that lurked in the shadows, was penetrating the enemy lines and showing the Germans who the boss really was.

On the Front Major Wood reported a new cheerfulness and quiet assurance from the men. We were now more active in artillery operations than the enemy and deserters from the German lines came in fairly often, which went a long way to raising the spirit of our troops. The deserters had letters in their possession that described the dire straits and economic pressure that Germany was under. He brought news from the Front directly from the mouths of the fighting men who said, 'The men at home who were unwilling to do their duty in the present crisis should have compulsory measures applied to them.'

And so a bill was passed through Parliament to that effect. Every single man between the ages of 18 and 41 who had no dependants was required to 'join up' at their first opportunity. There was no longer the option to shy away from the imposed responsibilities. There was a strong community feeling that those who were physically able should enlist and go to France to relieve the burden on the fighting troops.

It cannot have been easy for the men of Doncaster to summon up the courage to enlist, especially with such an ever-growing legacy of local dead and wounded. On Monday, 26 February 1917, information was received that Lieutenant C.R.F. Sandford MC, the youngest son of Archdeacon Sandford, Vicar of Doncaster, had been killed. In every newspaper that appeared there was page upon page of so-called 'Rolls of Honour'. The *Gazette* and *Chronicle* newspapers seemed to be evolving into giant obituaries and many of the townsfolk only read them to see who else had died while there must have been many others who tried to avoid reading them altogether.

The urgent need for more and more recruits and the pressure laid upon the men to join up, along with the emotional blackmail heaped upon them from friends, peers and families, was too much to bear for one individual, as the *Hull Daily Mail* of Friday, 3 August 1917 reports:

'Discharged Navy Man Called Up, Coroner's Strong Remarks.
'The Doncaster County Coroner held an inquest at Carcroft on Wednesday, on Arthur Percival (31), son of a miner, of 111 Markham Avenue, Carcroft, who stabbed himself twice over the heart with a pocket knife.'

Percival had been in the Navy but had been discharged because he was suffering from heart disease. Despite this, and because of the desperate state of the country, he was called up for military service. It must have been obvious to everyone apart from the army doctor that he ought not to have been called up in the first place, let alone now. The Coroner remarked, 'It amounted to public scandal, simply prompted by a desire to have every man in the army so long as he was of military age and could walk!' The jury returned a verdict of 'Suicide while temporarily insane' but with an advisory note protesting against the action of the military authorities. Arthur Percival could not bear the thought of being of no use to his fellow townsfolk and countrymen, his pride would not allow it.

We talk a lot about the men on the Front, the sons that followed them, the lads in training in readiness for their turn and those that were employed guarding our shores in Blighty. We mention the wives and daughters working hard to keep things together at home, and we document the arduous work of the temporary recruits in the local factories and industry. What of the boys who were too young to fight? What of the lads from the villages who were without their fathers, how were they faring? The majority of them were taking to their roles as 'men of the house' remarkably well. There existed a minority, however, that did not live up to their fathers' expectations. With little or no discipline and no father figure some boys went 'off the rails'.

In the Borough Court during May 1917 there were numerous cases involving juvenile offenders. Two boys were charged with stealing a 10-shilling treasury note and were bound over and ordered to pay the cost between them. One lad was sent to the reformatory for five years for stealing a shilling from a shop, a little harsh perhaps, but he had been bound over for a similar offence before and also had been birched. Two more youngsters were dealt with for breaking into a glass showcase. The elder culprit had recently been bound over for breaking a plate glass window in the town which cost £3 12s 6d and so he received six of the birch whereas his accomplice was bound over. Yet another case was brought against three more boys who were all bound over for stealing a glass bottle from a chemist's errand-boy. The previous week's hearings saw a 14-year-old Bentley pit pony driver receive a 20-shilling fine for his foul and abusive language. He was summoned under a breach of the Mines Act and was prosecuted by a Mr Allen for disobeying orders. Mr Allen also remarked, 'it brought into question whether the management and officials were going to run the pit, or the boys. When spoken to by a deputy the defendant turned out the most dreadful foul language'.

By way of a contrast however, the majority of the lads were conducting themselves properly and doing a sterling job of holding the fort and keeping the town ticking over. The older youths were setting a good example for the younger ones by working in the local mines in place of their fathers. In New Edlington, at the Yorkshire Main Colliery, one such boy was doing just that. It was March 1917 when the Doncaster Borough Coroner together with a jury at the Guildhall, French Gate, heard the case of John William Moffitt, a 16-year-old who had been killed while working at the Edlington mine. John was a 'rope-runner' and the son of Samuel Moffitt of 18 Princes Crescent, New Edlington. The enquiry was attended by Mr H. Danby, HM Inspector of Mines, Mr R. Clayton, the manager of the colliery, and Mr Woodward, representing the Edlington branch of the Yorkshire Miners Association. The fateful events were read out:

> 'The deceased went to work at 6 o'clock on the Saturday morning. At about half-past nine he was walking in front of a run of tubs. A girder across the roof which was holding up a pulley used in connection with the tubs, suddenly broke while the deceased was practically underneath, with the result that a large quantity of roof fell on the deceased, who was badly injured. He was got out of the pit, first aid was rendered, and he was conveyed to Doncaster Infirmary where he died at about a quarter to five on the same day.'

Samuel Moffitt, the boy's father, said that his son had worked at Yorkshire Main for about eighteen months and had been a rope runner for about four months. A witness who saw the boy after the accident and while in the ambulance on his way to the Infirmary said the boy had asked 'How did it happen?'

What makes the story more heart-rending is that the witness was Samuel, the boy's father, who had been working nearby at the time of the accident. Samuel recalled how he found a fall of dirt from the roof in a crossgate with the nearest tubs being about 40 yards away. He did not see his son at that time but, while he was examining the place, about half a tub of dirt fell and Samuel heard a moan. He shouted for assistance and it was only when the earth was moved that he found it to be his own son. 'He was laid in the middle of the road semi-conscious and he did not speak. He was bleeding at the back of the head. Between two and three tons of dirt had fallen and I found the broken girder, a steel one, with the rope and pulley still attached. The girder was there to carry the pulley and not to support the roof.'

Albert Roebuck, of Warmsworth Road, was the deputy. He reported to the court that he had examined the place before the accident and found everything was in working order but that afterwards he discovered that the girder had worn in one place, the part that had

William Morton Eden ©National Portrait Gallery.

broken. In his opinion it was the breaking girder that had caused the roof to fall. He said, 'It was a "weight bump" which caused the girder to break. There would have been nothing to warn the boy – it would have gone off suddenly, like a cannon.' Dr. Abrahams, the surgeon from the Doncaster Infirmary, advised that death was caused by shock, together with a fracture at the base of the skull, and compression of the brain. The verdict of Accidental Death was returned.

Around the same time came the sad news of the death of a local peer of the realm. Although having little or nothing to do with the war, it describes how one of the local villages came to be named. The death was that of Lord Auckland, after whom Auckland Road in the centre of town is named. William Morton Eden, 5th Baron Auckland, was the grandson of Mr John Walbanke Childers of Cantley Hall. William spent his early years living at Carr House (after which Carr House Road is named) before his father, the 4th

Baron, purchased an estate known as 'Streetthorpe' from a Mr Yarborough-Parker. William Eden was described as a stereotypical country gentleman caring not for the politics of the town but preferring the more leisurely approach to life, being content to spend his days relaxing on his rambling estate or helping out with church duties. He did have a part to play in the local community however, and was the chair of Armthorpe Parish Council for some time. Despite being a West Riding Magistrate for the Lower Strafforth and Tickhill Division, he was seldom seen on the bench at Doncaster or Thorne, and more rarely in Quarter Sessions. Shortly after the purchase of 'Streetthorpe' William's father used their surname 'Eden' to rename the estate 'Edenthorpe'. The name still exists today but it is more a housing estate than a rambling, picturesque, country one. One tenuous link to the war is that William's eldest son, and heir to the baronetcy, was killed in March 1915 while serving as Lieutenant in the King's Royal Rifle Corps.

During July 1917, Lieutenant A.N. Wills, who was the first secretary of the Volunteer movement, was in Doncaster on leave. He looked very fit and extremely bronzed after his eighteen months in the trenches. He had been extremely lucky, having sustained not even a scratch, and he was still wearing a wrist watch that Doncaster Corporation had presented to him when he had left the town to join the Army. To show off their expert gunmanship, A Company - Doncaster took part in a national shooting competition. A miniature range was set up and ten shots per contestant were allowed at a 1-inch bullseye.

The following scores (out of 100) are from local lads, demonstrating their accuracy, taken from that week's edition of the *Doncaster Chronicle*: Sergeant H. Pillin - 98; Private L. Tagg - 98; Sergeant F. Pearson - 97; Sergeant G. Wiles - 97; Lance-Corporal Crabtree - 96; Corporal Mandeville - 96; Private S. Webb - 95; Private H.C. Hill - 95; Quartermaster F.J. Clarke - 92; Corporal W. Allan - 92; Private G. Flintham - 92; Sergeant Waddington - 91; Private Dennis Cooke - 90; Private W. E. Clarke - 90; Corporal Everett - 90; Lieutenant T.L. Atkinson - 90; Private W. Marrison - 90; Private H. Moat - 84; Private W. Gilbert - 80, and Lance-Corporal Bond - 77. The average was 91 making their accuracy second to none.

The weekly orders came from Major M.E. Clark who was commanding the 19th Battalion of the West Riding Volunteers. Officers who were commanding companies were to arrange their own parades on Sunday 8 July, paying particular attention to bayonet fighting and extended order drill. D Company were to go to camp at Stapleton Park near Pontefract on Saturday 7 July for one night and two days. The mounted section of the Volunteers were told that they must parade on the Sunday at Butterbusk Farm, Conisbrough, at 10.30am. Happy news indeed that none of the companies were being sent across the sea to the 'mincing-machine' that was the Western Front.

Not so lucky though was Private Marlow of 27 The Crescent, Woodlands who was in No. 3 Canadian Casualty Clearing Station based in France suffering from serious injuries to the lower back which had penetrated his abdomen. He was brought in unconscious on 3 July 1917 but died the following day. The Chaplain wrote a letter to Mrs E. Marlow, the man's wife, stating that 'Private Marlow had fought a good fight and that he would be buried at a cemetery in France with due respect and military honours.' Marlow had done all he could to 'join up', undergoing two separate operations for varicose veins before the army would

Private Marlow.

accept him. As a coal miner at nearby Brodsworth Colliery he wasn't required to enlist but he did so anyway for King and Country. He was well known and liked in the vicinity of Woodlands and left behind his wife to care for their eight children. He was 37 years of age.

Almost as Private Marlow was taking his dying breath a family on the opposite side of town were celebrating. Captain James Crampton, a Hexthorpe soldier with the local KOYLI regiment, had been awarded the Military Cross for an act of gallantry at Hill 60, near Ypres. His family lived in Ramsden Road and were an old Hexthorpe family. Captain Crampton had been educated at Hexthorpe School under the Master, Mr Willing. In fact, Mr Willing was so elated on hearing the news of the decoration that he arranged for a 'little ceremony' at the school. Crampton's colleagues at The Plant railway works were happy to receive and congratulate him on his return to the village. That's what life was like for Doncastrians during the Great War. Those with reason to celebrate did so with a sheepish caution for fear of upsetting a neighbour who was lamenting a loss.

While the Crampton family were proudly attending the 'little ceremony', another Hexthorpe family from number 5 of the same street received the news of the death of their son. Private Herbert Cutts, aged 19, of the King's Own Yorkshire Light Infantry had met his death while in action in France. The sad news came directly from the War Office but was also conveyed in person by Lance-Corporal Downing of Earlesmere Avenue, Balby who was home on leave at the time. Downing spoke of his comrade Herbert Cutts, saying, 'Bert was always a cheery, willing soldier who will be sorely missed by the gun team and myself'. Young Cutts had enlisted on 3 September 1915 and was posted to France on 14 December 1916. He was killed instantly by an exploding shell. Before the outbreak of the war he had worked as a warehouseman for Howarth and Parkin's Chemists, Market Place, Doncaster.

The name of another Hyde Park lad was added to the Doncaster Roll of Honour in the same week. Sapper Harold Elvidge, aged 26, was killed while on active service in France. He was attached to DORE (Doncaster's Own Royal Engineers) and was the son of Mr George Elvidge of 40, Cunningham Road. Before joining up, he was an apprentice stonemason with Messrs Dennis Gill and Son, builders and contractors, Netherhall Road. And, as if Ramsden Road had not experienced enough sadness, this news was promptly followed by yet more. Mr and Mrs Cope of 2 Ramsden Road, opposite the home of Herbert Cutts, received chilling news from a lieutenant in their son's regiment. Private Bernard Cope, aged 23, of the Machine Gun Corps had enlisted on 14 August 1914, at the very outbreak of the war. He was a baker by trade and his father was a wheelwright for GNR (Great Northern Railway). He was acting as cook to the officers' mess while they were under a very heavy enemy bombardment during which he was 'hit and killed instantaneously by a shell'. The lieutenant went on to describe Bernard as, 'a hard and conscientious worker and his good work in and out of the line has often been brought to my notice'. Bernard was posted to France on 13 April 1915 and had a brother who was serving in the RFA. Lads that led by example in their respective villages seemed to receive more recognition at the end than others. The fact that they answered the call to arms quickly was exploited by the local media to encourage those that were unsure of whether to enlist themselves.

On the far side of Doncaster, in the quaint village of Arksey, Mr and Mrs Richard Leadbeater of Stone Cottages, were dealt their share of the heartbreak. The headlines read, 'TWO BRAVE ARKSEY BOYS - The First to Enlist, Now Dead'. Lance-Corporal Albert Leadbeater had been killed in September 1916 around the same time that his brother George, a private in the KOYLI, had been badly wounded in the shoulder, spending eleven months in hospital and at home. George was declared fit for battle again and returned to the Front in June 1917. He had been 'picked up unconscious in the field' by the RAMC suffering from severe shrapnel wounds to the head, chest and legs. He never regained consciousness and died without leaving a message for his loved ones. He was buried on the same day in a Military Cemetery in France. The news of his death was received by his wife who had to find the words to inform their 'little child'.

The *Doncaster Chronicle* goes on to say:

'Both brothers were well known in the village and will be remembered with fondness at Bentley Colliery where they had worked. They were happy, jovial lads who were liked by everybody, and the fact that they were the very first two to enlist at Arksey, in September 1914, adds to the great sacrifice they have made. George, the eldest son, was 28-years-old, and Albert, who was killed a year ago, was the second son, and was 23 and unmarried. A memorial service will be held at Arksey Church on Sunday afternoon at half-past three.'

As the war escalated it is difficult to balance out the grief with stories of happiness as the newspapers were packed, cover to cover, with terrible news. It is with this thought in mind then that I make no apology for illustrating that fact within the pages of this book, it is the best way to demonstrate the losses that this town felt almost one hundred years ago. Death was so rife on the Western Front that no family was safe to celebrate for very long. Every community lived in fear of the next influx of terrible news.

Not all losses were caused by the enemy however. One such accident that was a direct result of the war but not at the hands of the enemy was the loss of the ship HMS *Vanguard*. During the night of 9 July 1917 a stockpile of cordite, a version of gun-powder, caught fire and exploded. The ship sank almost instantly killing 804 crew. To this day, the incident remains the largest loss of life caused by an accidental explosion in the history of the United Kingdom, and certainly one of the worst accidental losses of the Royal Navy. As a result of the explosion, Mr and Mrs R.J. Graham, of Hall Gate received the sad news of the death by drowning of their son, First Class Boy J.W. Graham, aged 17.

J.W. Graham - HMS Vanguard.

One tradition that commenced as a direct result of the loss of life was that of erecting street shrines. There had been one unveiled by the residents of Bentley and then, a few days later, another by the residents of Elmfield Road in Hyde Park. The initial idea came from a Mrs Goforth but the plans were seen to fruition by the support of a Mrs Calder who had a strong connection with the area and the community. There were 37 names on the list, with a couple of families refusing to give consent for their sons' names to be included. The flags of the Allies were worked around the border of the tablet with an image of the crucifixion at the top. The tablet was unveiled by the Reverend J.R.F. Frazer, Vicar of Christ Church, one Sunday afternoon in September 1917 in the presence of a large gathering. A procession had been formed outside Christ Church on Thorne Road before setting off to Elmfield Road. Along the route the choir sang the Litany and, on arrival at the shrine, they sang 'Oh God Our Help in Ages Past', before Psalm 91 was given in a Gregorian chant. The shrine was sprinkled with holy water as the pungent odour of incense hung in the air.

The vicar then read out the names on the shrine: Mr Armfield; E. Beckwith; F. Beckwith; A. Blackburn; D. Calder; H.P. Calder; A.C. Camsill; W. Eland; Mr Garnett; C.H. Garnet; T.R. Goforth; B. Hawes; J. Hawes; G. Jackson; J. Maw; R.W. Morton; F. Needham; W. Nichols; W. H. Richardson; P. Richardson; W.B. Richardson; P. Rodwell; R. Saverall; H. Smith; S. Sprakes; W. Stocks; H. Tipper; J. G. Trout; H. Vaughan; M.L. Vaughan; T.W. Vaughan; J. Vinan; E. J. Ward; H. Wigglesworth; Alfred Wigglesworth; P. Wigglesworth, and P. R. Wilson.

After a short silence he led into his sermon with these words, 'God has laid this war upon us to call us to the true worship of Himself. Let us see to it that we practise the religion that we profess. How many of you have been confirmed and been told what to do but have never carried out what you have promised? The nation has moved away from Divine will and the war was God's way of bringing us back in line, God has always dealt that way with those who have forsaken him. Take your prayer books and see what you were called upon to do. Unless the present state of religion is remedied, this war will go on. God will leave us at war until we return to him.'

Controversially, the vicar evidently saw the Great War as a punishment from God or perhaps it was an ingenious way of swelling the audience for his Sunday services. Religion did play a part in the war and perhaps every country and ethnic background involved in it, friend or foe, would have been given a similar lecture from their clergy.

And now, as Christmas 1917 approached and another year of bloody fighting was drawing to a close, many Doncaster folk were beginning to wonder if the war would ever end. What commenced as an 'in and out' battle a little over three years previously had dragged on and on, taking with it almost an entire generation of men. There were still a great many soldiers being accommodated in Doncaster, men from other towns throughout the whole country. How were they to enjoy a traditional family Christmas? This chapter ends with a call to the kind-hearted residents of this town to open their doors to the lonely stranger during the season of good will.

'THE HOME FIRESIDE FOR SOLDIERS AT CHRISTMAS - A Letter to the Editor of the *Doncaster Chronicle*, December 1917.

'Dear Sir, most of your readers will have some of their family at Christmas time, far away from the old log fireside and home gathering, and it may be that while they have sent the familiar parcel of 'extras' for their husband, sweetheart, or boy, they would like to fill the vacant chair by another Khaki Boy. If such readers will notify me of any hospitality they would like to offer, stating number of guests, and whether Christmas Day or Boxing Day, for dinner or tea, or both, their name and address plainly to 10 Waterdale, on or before Friday 21 December, I shall perhaps be able to assist them in making happy through their kindness, some of the many soldiers billeted in our town. Those soldiers, while they will no doubt be provided with extra Christmas fare, will miss the home comforts which your readers can give.

'On behalf of the War Emergency Council, yours faithfully, F.J. Stoker - YMCA hut, Waterdale.'

CHAPTER 5

Nearing the End

As another Christmas came and went and the previous year's losses slipped slowly from vivid memory, Doncastrians found themselves no better off for the New Year that was upon them. They had smiled in the face of adversity but must have wondered how many more lives would need to be sacrificed in order to gain the victory so desperately desired?

The previous year had ended with the Mayor of Doncaster, Councillor Abner Carr, losing his youngest son, Private Harold D. Carr, in the bloodbath. He had hoped that a discrepancy with the official report, whereby the regimental number was incorrect, would mean that there was some sort of mix-up. But alas, there was not. Private Carr, 32-years-old, who was educated at Mr Jackson's School on Hall Gate, was attached to the Sherwood Forresters where he saw active service in a number of countries. Latterly, he had been engaged in chasing Turks somewhere in Palestine. He had written to his father to tell him this on 17 November 1917. However, by the time his letter had arrived at the Mansion House he had already been dead for about a fortnight. The Mayor refused to allow his bereavement to interfere with his official duties saying, 'I am only one of the thousands similarly bereaved and it would meet my wishes if no more prominence was given to my loss than to that of any other person. It is no greater because I happen to be the Mayor of Doncaster.'

Food, or the lack of it, had been a problem throughout these times of austerity and 1918 was no exception. One of the opening articles in the first Doncaster newspaper of the New Year carried the headline:

'DONCASTER IN WAR TIME - There was very little beef in the hands of butchers for the weekend trade at Doncaster last Saturday, and the mutton obtainable was not sufficient to go round. Most of the butchers kept their shops closed all day on Saturday until after their regular customers had been supplied. Many people were unable to obtain any serviceable joint for the Sunday dinner, and rabbits went up to 3s. 6d. each.'

That year also saw a return of the dreaded potato blight. Potatoes were always a cheap way to fill the hungry stomachs of many a tired soldier or hard working miner. In many households they took the place of good meat. The year commenced with an important message and vital advice for all the allotment holders and gardeners in the town from the Food Production Department. Everyone that could was encouraged to sow a larger crop and to pay particular attention to cultivation and spraying during the winter months. The department also set about educating growers on the effective use of preventative sprays that would help to keep 'the blight' at bay. The County Organiser for Spraying, Mr N.P. Chamney, began to make arrangements for local lectures and information on the subject. Emphasizing the point, the Food Production Department announced, 'You cannot afford to throw away food while it is dear and while the nation needs it so much. Every particle of food wasted helps Germany, and every particle saved helps England. Which will you help?' The Mayor of Doncaster, Councillor Abner Carr, followed this up with a meeting held at the Palace Theatre one Sunday night. Referring to the shortage of food and to the queues of people in the town on Saturdays he said it was up to the people to make the best of things. The authorities were doing and would do everything they could to assist everyone but he asked that the public should also assist the authorities.

A little later, during February 1918, the subject of the food shortage appeared in the local press. A small representative committee from the villages of Bentley-with-Arksey and Adwick-le-Street travelled to London to put their case before the Ministry of Food. They carried an urgent request from the two villages that the food supply of the Doncaster area be increased. The Food Control Committees of Doncaster Borough and Rural District were also invited to join the plea. The requests of the two committees were heard with success. The

Ministry immediately acknowledged that the current meat ration of ½lb per head per week was insufficient for a miner to work on and promised to endeavour to increase the supply of meat to ¾lb during the following week. All classes of the community were to benefit from the increase, not just the miners. Even better, the Ministry of Food promised to raise the ration further over the coming weeks to 1½lbs per head per week.

Some of the villagers were being quite resourceful with the way they shared out the food, so much so that they were praised by the Corporation and held up as an example to others. One innovative way of stretching out the supply came in the form of communal kitchens and was first introduced in Carcroft and Woodlands Model Village. The kitchens are described quite romantically in the week's press:

'The savoury odours of the various dishes floated out on the noon-day air, and the miners' wives trudged in with jugs and basins. A typical menu consists of: soup 1½d per portion; fish cakes 2d each, bean and macaroni pies 3d each, savoury stew 4d, potatoes 1d per portion, mashed swedes 1d per portion, jam pudding 2d and milk puddings 1½d per portion. The menus are varied day by day.'

On the opening day at Carcroft 530 portions of food were sold, the next day 680, followed by 418, 413, and 429, the kitchens only being open from 11.30am until 2.30pm daily. The official Carcroft opening was undertaken in the drizzling rain by Mrs J. H. Pawson standing in for Mrs Humble who had the 'flu. The Bullcroft Ambulance Band made music as the Union Jack floated from the kitchen roof. Mr Blunt, manager of Bullcroft Colliery, was in attendance along with Mr Davidson, chairman of Adwick-le-Street Urban District Council, and many representatives from the local clergy. The amount of food sold at Woodlands was even higher – such was the crush every day that the police had to be called in to regulate the queue. The great thing about these communal kitchens was that they were not governed by the rationing so that as long as you had the money to pay for it, you could order as much food as you wanted, there being no maximum limit. In many ways they resembled a colliery canteen in that, after paying for the food, customers progressed down the counter being served with each item before arriving at the far end with the full quota. At Carcroft a purpose built building was erected solely for the kitchen, whereas at Woodlands the kitchen was set up in the basement of the Drill Hall. The schemes were fully backed by the Urban District Council and the colliery companies and were sincerely appreciated by the townsfolk.

During May, as the air was beginning to warm into British summertime, the need for more volunteers continued. One gentleman wrote to the editor of the *Doncaster Chronicle* with an urgent appeal for volunteers which begs the question: if he was so concerned about the lack of troops, why hadn't he joined up himself? The final part of his letter reads:

'Are you going to take the risk of being "too late" for the sake of a few hours of work each month which you will thoroughly enjoy once you try it? God help England if the volunteers are required! Your country asks you to volunteer to defend your home if and when invasion should come, so that many soldiers (who have already undergone their training in readiness for fighting at the Front) may take their place alongside the lads in France. Do you begrudge these lads their reinforcements? Do you begrudge a copper for those who have given so much fine gold for you? The honour and life of your mother, wife, or sister may depend on you being an efficient volunteer.'

Was this intended to generate a feeling of guilt and obligation amongst the lads who had not yet fully committed to the cause, even after four years of watching their fellow citizens do their duty? Major M.E. Clark, the Commander of the 19th Battalion (Doncaster) West Riding Volunteer Regiment, strategically placed the battalion's weekly orders directly under the letter which went as follows:

'Parades for Sunday, 5 May 1918, A and C Companies will fire part 2 of the Efficients' Annual Musketry Course on the Cantley Range commencing at 11am. The second in command will visit Rossington. A class of instruction on the subject of "Musketry" for officers will be held at the Drill Hall, French Gate commencing on Friday evening, 3 May at 7.30pm. Railway warrants for outlying detachments to travel on will be issued from the Battalion Orderly Room. Arrangements have been made to hold a camp from Saturday 18 until Tuesday, 21 May. The camp will comprise of the 16th, 17th, 18th and 19th Battalions of the West Riding Volunteers and will be accommodated at Redmires, near Sheffield.'

That all sounded quite an enjoyable programme of events, rather like Boy Scouts for grown ups. I wonder how many men joined up as an immediate response to both the letter and the Battalion Orders?

Before recounting this next story I must stress that by far the vast majority of Doncastrians gave the war effort their full and wholehearted support, both morally and financially. Whenever there was a new scheme to raise money for either the troops themselves or for one of the many by-products of the war, the people rallied around. There was however, as there is today and probably always will be, a small minority who saw a gap in the 'criminal' market and sought out new ways to exploit others' good nature for their own gain. On Montagu Street in Doncaster a young private by the name of Robert Barker, of the Durham Light Infantry, was going from door to door collecting money in aid of the wounded soldiers who were currently residing at the Arnold Military Hospital. At number 110 lived Police Constable Fox with his wife. His wife had noticed the private visiting the neighbours and informed her husband of that fact, at which point PC Fox watched from the window as the soldier called at several houses receiving money before pretending to enter the amounts into a pocket book. After a short while the man came to his house and said, 'I am collecting money on behalf of the wounded soldiers at Arnold's Hospital who are having an entertainment at the Corn Exchange on Monday next.'

PC Fox asked if the man was at Arnold Hospital himself to which he replied that he was not. The PC went on to ask whether he had written authority to collect for Arnold Hospital to which the man also answered no. Private Barker was then promptly arrested. At the later court hearing it transpired that the fraud had been going on for quite some time and, at the time of his arrest, Barker had a little over eight shillings in 'small money' on his person. Mrs Pickering, the Commandant at Arnold Hospital, was called in to identify Private Barker but could not on account of never having seen him before. It also came to light that he had no financial reason for stooping so low as he was not poor. He had married the daughter of a Balby farmer named Berry. His wife was living in Regent Street while he resided in Woodfield Lane. Private Robert Barker had been in trouble with the law before also, for on 15 April 1915 he had been sentenced in the same court to three months' hard labour for assaulting a female. For this charge he was committed to gaol for three months.

Others were letting the side down too as another story illustrates, this time from the village of Highfields. John Smith, a coal miner from nearby Brodsworth colliery, and his wife, Hannah, were summoned to the West Riding Police Court by the complainant, Amelia McGarry, on a charge of assault. Hannah Smith also entered a counter summons against Amelia McGarry on the same charge. Mrs McGarry of 84 Coppice Road gave her evidence saying, 'On 7 June 1918 my husband and Mr Smith were talking outside the house about a quarrel that had occurred in February. I went out to see them and Mr Smith said that he would give me what I wanted. As soon as my husband's back was turned he struck me a severe blow to the side of the head, which needed medical attendance, and then Mrs Smith and her sister both got hold of me and gave me a thrashing.' In cross examination she denied that she had assaulted Mrs Smith, which claim was backed up by several witnesses. Mr Smith denied the charge saying, 'Mrs McGarry rushed at my wife and delivered two blows, my wife retaliated and I just left them to fight it out.' Mrs McGarry did not deny this. After hearing several other witnesses the magistrates bound the two women over to keep the peace for six months or else receive a fine of £5 each. Mr Smith was fined 40 shillings for striking Mrs McGarry. The Chairman, Brigadier-General Bewicke-Copley, of Sprotbrough Hall, stressed that under no circumstances, no matter what the provocation, should a man strike a woman.

Finally on this theme there comes an item from the quintessential country village of Arksey and a headline in the *Doncaster Gazette* which read:

'Woman Fined for Assault - At Doncaster on Saturday, May Drew, a single young woman, summoned Mary A. Gretton, married, of Askern, for assault. It was alleged that the defendant struck the complainant across the face, thrashed, and kicked her until she fell to the ground unconscious. A Special Constable picked her up. In defence, Mrs Gretton said that the girl had provoked her by pulling faces, putting her fingers to her nose, and calling her names. A fine of 40 shillings was imposed.'

It really was a gritty existence in the mining villages of Doncaster!

Meanwhile in August 1918 the Volunteer Battalion were persevering with their training, as the following article demonstrates quite well:

'The topic is all of the camp at Burton Agnes. The advance party under Captain Cooke went on Wednesday and the main body go on Saturday, leaving Doncaster at 3:30pm in the afternoon. Burton Agnes is a little village five or six miles outside Bridlington. This is the first time the battalion has had two proper camps in the same year, and in view of the weather we are now having, the men are looking forward to it as a holiday recreation. The camp is to last for a full week and the programme includes an afternoon's sports gala. One of the volunteers, Sergeant Higgins, is now a fully qualified camp cook, he won his spurs at Firbeck – if a cook may be said to win spurs – and there will be no holding him now he is the proud possessor of a certificate from the School of Cookery at York.'

It was a hard life for those volunteers!

With good news from France being replaced with even better news each day, the threat of invasion was diminishing. One by one the various powers were busy either demobilizing their armies or fighting for an armistice. For the first time since the war had started whole empires were working together, not to formulate master plans to over-run the Allied forces, but on how best to put forward agreements that would end the bloodshed once and for all. One decisive battle for the British Army came on 19 September 1918 at the Battle of Megiddo. We were destined to win at the start but we were not going to let complacency ruin our chances. We, along with the Allied Egyptian Expeditionary Force (EEF) went head to head against the Ottoman Yildirim Army Group, which consisted of three armies each the strength of barely an Allied corps. The British and Indian infantry broke through enemy lines, thousands of prisoners were taken into custody and a great many miles of territory were captured by the Allies. The British Commander of the EEF, General (later Field Marshal) E.H.H. Allenby, later said, 'I desire to convey to all ranks of all arms of the force under my command my admiration and thanks for their great deeds of the past week, and my appreciation of their gallantry and determination, which have resulted in the total destruction of the VII and the VIII Turkish Armies opposed to us. Such a complete victory has seldom been known in all the history of war.'

At a meeting held in the Mansion House in September 1918, Mr Abner Carr, the Mayor of Doncaster, was busy organizing a shipment of parcels for prisoners of war. It was decided to fix the radius of appeal to the public at nine miles. The fund was to be registered as 'The Doncaster and District Prisoners of War Fund.' A Flag Day was organized for a Saturday in September, almost to the day when the parents of Seaman Samuel (Bob) Saveall, RND, of 54 Elmfield Road, Hyde Park, Doncaster received news from him that he was a prisoner of war. He had been reported missing on 25 March and had written his letter from Güstrow, Mecklenburg on 25 May. The letter, which was addressed to his sister and had taken four months to arrive, made an urgent appeal for smoking materials. He had joined up three years before, having previously been employed as a grocer's assistant with Messrs Hodgson and Hepworth.

On 25 September 1918 a group of German prisoners of war arrived at Doncaster Railway Station under escort. They had been transferred to the borough to work on farmland at Warmsworth. A fairly large number of locals had turned out to witness their arrival but there was no demonstration of any kind. The 1916-17 report from the Yorkshire Miners' Association was issued by Mr John Wadsworth MP, which highlighted the good work that had been done by German prisoners working down local mines. With the lesser wages and costs, together with conditions that were worse than normal, the Germans had allowed for collieries in the district to be 'opened out'.

No. 3 Volunteer Battalion KOYLI were once again under canvas as they left Doncaster for one week of training at Burton Agnes, just outside Bridlington. The camp was under the brigade command of Colonel Hall-Dalwood of Sheffield and the KOYLI lads were under the command of Major M.E. Clark. There was a full and comprehensive programme of hard but interesting work including night training exercises. Because of a period of extremely inclement weather the boys were happy to be home afterwards. The weather in Doncaster was a little better with isolated showers giving way to warm summer sunshine. Making the most of it a good number of Doncaster folk braved the rigours of wartime travel bound for Scarborough, Bridlington, Cleethorpes, and other seaside resorts on the east and west coasts. Those who stayed at home found a variety of attractions on offer in the town. There were fund-raising events for the Balby and Arnold Hospitals; a show and sports at Woodlands; Sandall Beat, Hexthorpe Flats, and Edlington Wood beauty spots and the beauty of the Don Gorge at Sprotbrough. There was a garden fete organised by the RAOB (Royal Antediluvian Order of Buffaloes) at Askern, the venue being the bowling green of the Swan Hotel, on behalf of the Blinded Soldiers Fund. There was a bowling contest; Professor Jakes, conjuror and illusionist; George Anelay, facial contortionist; and a pianoforte recital by Mr Douglas Brown. In the evening Springett's Quadrille Band played for dancing on the green until dusk and then later in the Swan Hotel ballroom.

It is August 1918 and with the benefit of hindsight we know that the bloodshed is soon to end, Doncastrians one hundred years ago, however, did not. For all they knew, the war would continue indefinitely. In these final weeks the killing continued as much as it always had, there were victories, but still many casualties including Lance Corporal John Ardron of the King's Own Yorkshire Light Infantry, of 80 Wheatley Lane, who was recovering in a Manchester hospital from a bullet wound to the right shoulder and Private James Glover Stafford, of Bentley Road, who was reported killed in action. He had worked in the offices of the Bentley-with-Arksey Urban District Council.

Others included Private S.H. Lawson, West Yorkshire Regiment, of 70 Littlemoor Lane, Balby, who had only been at the Front since April 1918, was killed. He had worked as a baker at Mr Bloxham's on Union Street. Lance-Corporal Charles Carwall, Lincolnshire Regiment died of his wounds at a field ambulance station in France. He was 20 years of age and the only son of Mr H. Carwall, the Steward of Bentley West End Club. The soldier had suffered five rejections before he was finally accepted into the army!

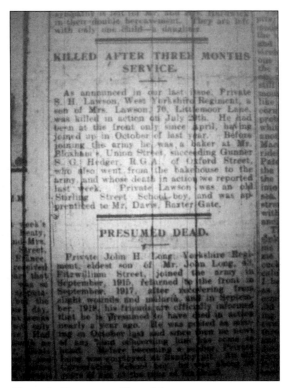

From the Doncaster Chronicle.

Another was Sergeant Walter Gleadhall, Dorsetshire Regiment, of 38 Bridge Street, Hexthorpe, who was severely gassed and wounded in action on 8 November. He had worked at Brodsworth Main Colliery and had a wife and six young children.

On 11 November 1918, the guns fell silent and the silence was deafening. At the Front our men's ears were still ringing with the thud of the German guns, and at home our minds and hearts were still reeling from the aftermath. The victory was celebrated in style. An anouncement was made from the Mansion House steps by the Mayor and Civic party and the whole town listened to the Armistice address:

'It needs to be written in measure of poetry and chanted as a psalm of thanksgiving to a setting of the most majestic music. The souls of men cannot be otherwise satisfied, they are bursting

The Mayor's speech from the Mansion House steps.

to find an expression. The story of these mighty events, nevertheless, has to be related in such ways and forms as are available to ordinary mortals, even though it should fail to satisfy, on account of its inadequacies of expression, both the writer and the reader.

'What a wonderful, what a still almost unbelievable story it is! The war is over and the world has peace in its stead. The war is over, and its authors are laid in the dust. The war is over, and they that took to the sword have perished by the sword. Peace is with us, and it is to be a clean peace. The world hereafter is to become safe for democracy, for right has triumphed over might and moral force over brutal force. Prussian Militarism which has had the whole of civilization in its grip, a life or death grip, for four years and more, has failed in its avowed purpose and has been discredited and destroyed. The dragon of blood and iron has been slain! The war is over and the treaty-breakers have themselves been broken. The blasphemous Kaiser, who has so frequently made God in his own devilish image to suit his own wicked purposes and serve his own evil ends, has been driven into exile by his own people. The scabbard-rattlers are today quaking in their jack-boots. We [Doncaster] has been delivered from the armed tyranny that has so long oppressed it.

'It remains for those who have survived the appalling trials to make their own conduct both in the present and in the future worthy of the price that has been paid by the heroic lads who have fallen in the fray!'

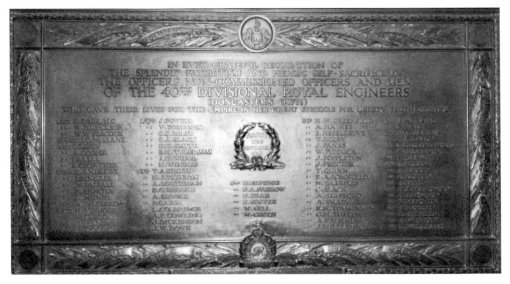

War Memorial in the Mansion House foyer.

Doncaster threw itself with exuberant joy into the celebration of one of the happiest days that the younger citizens of the town had ever known. The town was a sea of flags and all shops that kept such symbols of patriotism in stock did not have them for very long. The whole population invaded the streets for the day. The children marched jubilantly around waving the Union Flag and shouting themselves hoarse at the coming of a peace that was to thousands of them an unknown experience. Fireworks were let off with the additional relish of an exercise which had been under a ban, even on the time-honoured 5 November. Soldiers and their friends made the streets echo with the singing of songs made almost sacred by the associations of the 'long, long trail' to a 'Tipperary' which had seemed a million miles away only a few days previously. Here and there there were those who had consumed a little more alchohol than was necessary but there was no wild horseplay, no midnight tom-foolery, nothing but a liberal display of high spirits and of hearty, healthy satisfaction that 'the day' had finally arrived.

In 1909, prior to the outbreak of the Great War, 5 KOYLI had presented their new colours to the then Mayor, Councillor Bennett, and the Corporation for safe keeping and it was now time for those colours to be returned. At a ceremony held at the Mansion House the new Mayor, Councillor Jackson, handed over the two handsome banners to the battalion. Captain W. Lindsay Crawford MC, Second Lieutenant J. Stansfield MC, Sergeant Calvert VC, MM (Conisborough), together with Colonel Somerville and Sergeant Westlake MM represented the rest of the boys by taking the colours into their possession. The ceremony was accompanied by the KOYLI band and members of 3rd Volunteer Battalion who lined up in front of the Mansion House, flanked by thousands of local residents. The Mayor said:

> 'We are proud to have been chosen as custodian of the Colours and it is with the greatest of pleasure that we hand them back to you today on account of the grand record that you have brought with you of your deeds on foreign shores. We are pleased that this long, arduous, and exacting war has come to an end, and that the town of Doncaster has done its 'bit'. As the Chief Citizen, I heartily welcome you as worthy representatives of the men who answered the call in the early days of the War, when our Army numbered so few, and when we were so unprepared numerically for war. We have read of the doings of the Doncaster boys and we have always been proud of you. We now rejoice together that the black clouds of war have been lifted and the Armistice has been signed, and we are looking forward to a peace that should be clean, just, and permanent.'

Over the ensuing weeks men trickled back to Doncaster to be with their loved ones once again and with them they brought amazing stories of heroism and bravery. Some brought tales of hardship, particularly those who had been captured by the Germans. Bombardier Boothman, of Penistone Street, Wheatley said of his experience:

'We were treated like dogs, being marched for miles to a railway terminus. After we had been transported we again had to march 40 kilometres to the prison camp. Many men passed out on the way and were left to die by the roadside. When at the camp we were brutally treated with excessive task work and starvation. We were given a handful of broken wheat which had been made into a wretched sort of bread. No fatty food was ever given, milk was unknown, and meat was a rarity. The bread was too hard and crusty for some of the sick prisoners to eat and the crusts thrown aside were carefully salvaged, and when a sufficient quantity had accumulated a few currants were added and the combination was made into a feeble sort of plum duff.'

The conditions under which the prisoners existed must have been horrific as throughout the winter months of 1917-18 they were housed in simple bell tents while the snow on the other side of the canvas sometimes drifted up to four feet. There were twelve men to a tent and there was only one blanket issued to every three men. Requests for warm clothing were ignored and supplies sent from their families back in Doncaster were looted before they arrived. Out of the 2,800 prisoners in Bombardier Boothman's camp only 300 survived to tell the tale.

As the large scale celebrations subsided and the private celebrations continued, as families grieved behind closed doors and attempted to make sense of the previous years' events and as soldiers returning from the fight were constantly being reunited with their wives and children, the town began to turn its attention to the ways in which they would honour the fallen. In towns and villages across the land, monuments were being erected in grateful recognition and Doncaster was no exception. In Balby, a scheme was introduced and a committee formed to commemorate those men of the village who had fallen by way of a memorial. It was to be, 'quite undenominational, and free from all party and sect'.

Ideas were being thrashed about in the Corporation chamber on how best to incorporate a war memorial within the designs for the new Infirmary. Some councillors wanted to depict scenes of the war in a sculptured frieze along the top of the building, while others wanted to erect a stand-alone monument on the lawn in front of the Infirmary, one which could be easily visible from the road. Mr J. Swift of

Proposed Monument for the Royal Infirmary.

Doncaster designed the monument in the illustration which was to be 20ft in height with four steps leading up to it. The full description reads: 'The width of the base above the steps is eight feet. The plan is square with projected corners and at each corner above the scrolls is a figure typifying Grief, Consolation, Famine, and Hope. On the four faces of the monument are panels with ornamental swags and cherubs. Above the panels are a series of mouldings, and immediately above those are four niches, in which are figures of soldiers, representing the four Great Powers of Britain, France, Italy, and the United States. Over the figures are a further series of mouldings and ornamentation with what is suggested as shields on the four sides, with the insignia of local regiments that have distinguished themselves in the war. Surmounting

Memorial at St Jude's Church, Hexthorpe ©www.doncasterhistory.co.uk

the whole is a figure of Peace.' It truly was to be a grand monument to the town's fallen soldiers. Nevertheless, the plan to erect it never materialized, as any Doncastrian today will know.

St Jude's Church, in Hexthorpe, had their war memorial scheme in place too. From a January edition of the 1919 *Doncaster Chronicle* comes this headline and article:

'St Jude's Memorial Scheme, controversy at annual meeting.

'The first Annual General Meeting of parishioners in connection with the St Jude's Church, Hexthorpe, Memorial Hall Scheme was held on Monday evening in the schoolroom, Shadyside, the Vicar, Reverend A.J. Marrs presided. Miss Youdan, acting secretary, gave the accounts for the year, and announced that so far, with concerts etc., over £100 had been collected for the Memorial Hall Fund but £5,000 was the sum needed. The Vicar said he hoped to have a curio exhibition about March 13 or 15 to swell the proceeds for the Hall. Several persons had and were kindly offering curios for the occasion. The Vicar's warden, Mr Warner, proposed a vote of thanks to Miss Youdan for her willing work in connection with the scheme, which the Vicar seconded, and it was passed unanimously.

'Unfortunately for the scheme opinions were divided and quite an unusual amount of controversy was shown at the meeting. Mr F. Hemstock proposed that the money should be invested in buying a house for the curate. The Vicar outlined some of the objections pointing out that if the curate left, the house could be empty for many weeks. Then again, if the succeeding curate was unmarried he might not wish to live in a house, but prefer rooms. Mr S. Adams, a discharged young soldier, wished to know why so many of the principal public men in Hexthorpe were opposed to such a scheme as a Memorial Hall that was in memory of local fallen soldiers, and Mr Marrs said that he himself had been a long time trying to understand that, but had failed. The lack of support was deplorable. Mr F. Trolley, another discharged soldier and member of the Church, thought that the War Memorial scheme should be kept apart from the religious and church connotations. The Vicar pointed out that

All Saints Church, Woodlands.

not all of the £5,000 was to be raised in Hexthorpe as Mr Gresley [of railway fame] had promised to put the matter before his board, other businesses were to help with the fund, and Archdeacon Sandford, Vicar of Doncaster, had promised a grant of £350 towards the cost.'

The need for a new hall was apparent. Some members wanted it to be called the St Jude's Memorial Hall while others wished it to be named the St Jude's Parochial Hall. Whatever the name was to be was fairly irrelevant for the important aspect was that a new hall was needed. The schoolroom was completely inappropriate for prayer meetings, it being attached to a games room. One of the assembled party remarked, 'Prayer meetings are an impossibility with billiard balls clicking in the rear!'

The War Memorial for the Woodlands Colliery Village was to take the form of an open four-faced clock which was to be fixed in the church tower together with a tablet inside the church inscribed with the

Highfields Clock Tower ©www.doncasterhistory.co.uk

names of the fallen, while the nearby village of Highfields, built to house workers for the same Brodsworth Colliery, presented a multitude of ideas for ways in which to honour the fallen which included housing for the soldiers, baths, and a memorial hall. None of these materialized, however a clock tower was later provided at the entrance to the estate as a monument to the local men.

Every village in Doncaster, together with the town itself, played their part by erecting memorials to the fallen. Doncastrians wanted to remember their brave boys for eternity and for their children and grandchildren to remember them too, as they still do every year. As the year of the war's end passed they looked to 1919 for new life, new hope, and new opportunity and were provided with just that as a brighter and better town emerged from the horrors of the war years.

CHAPTER 6

The Settling Dust

During the early months of 1919, Doncaster folk struggled to get used to the fact that a great many of their loved ones were never coming home. Single parent families were now plentiful as mothers and daughters worked hard to keep things together in the home. Boys followed in their fathers' pre-war footsteps by taking their places at the local coal mines. The town was divided into two halves. There were those who wanted to remember the fallen in every aspect of life, and others who wanted to forget the misery as much as possible. In an effort to forget Doncastrians threw themselves into celebrations of one sort or another, celebrations impossible during the war years.

In the spring they welcomed the horse home to the green lanes of the racecourse having almost forgotten what it was like to see the horses with their riders. It was the first equestrian event since the St Leger race of 1914 and the town was crowded, the Corporation already having made preparations for dealing with a crowd double that of any spring meeting before the war. The streets were packed, and tramcars with their six-penny fares carried the visitors to the course. Tipsters and bookies descended upon the town and the streets took on the well known 'horsey' appearance associated only with the races. The Borough Magistrates had granted special drinks licenses at the Borough Courts for the two race days allowing the public houses to remain open all day, in the morning for non-intoxicants, and in the afternoon and evening for all drinks.

After the spring race meeting came Whitsuntide, and what a Whit week it turned out to be. Record crowds descended on Doncaster and the surrounding district making it the brightest holiday since 1914. As a direct reaction to the depressing years of the war the public were now entering with zest into everything of a pleasurable nature. The weather was tremendous and the town was full of great crowds, full of good humour. Both Whit Sunday and Whit Monday were beautiful days, the streets were thronged with people and the highways were alive with traffic. Luxurious charabancs were met with on every main road delivering tourists to Doncaster from many districts. Miners, mill-hands, iron-workers and representatives of all industries from all parts of Yorkshire came to Doncaster and surrounding areas on Whit Monday, enjoying a tour in the car. At Woodlands Model Village athletic sports in connection with the football club drew a great crowd; at Owston there was a garden fete; at Bawtry a garden fete and victory fair took place in aid of the Church Endowment Fund; at Edenthorpe there was a Boy Scouts' encampment and sports; at Doncaster the RSPCA organized a horse and vehicle parade, cycle, and fancy dress carnival and at night the Comrades of the Great War held a comic band contest. There certainly was no shortage of things to do and see. Hundreds of people flocked to the local beauty spots of Sandall Beat, the Race Common, Hexthorpe Flatts, Edlington Woods, Conisborough Castle, Roche Abbey, the Dukeries and so forth. The Grand Theatre, The Palace and The Picture Palace all had the same tale to tell.

At Arksey there was an impressive service attended by the Bishop of Sheffield as their take on a War Memorial was unveiled. The monument came in the form of the Peace Bells. The quaint village was surrounded on three of its sides by the growing industrialisation of the district, with the remaining side opening out through lovely old lanes and bridlepaths over a wide stretch of pasture and arable lands. Even now in the twenty-first century it still possesses a certain amount of seclusion and, in many ways, has the feel of a semi-rural hamlet. It was still very much a traditional village during the Great War years and so it came as no surprise that while the rest of the town were enjoying the hedonistic pleasures of Whit Monday, the villagers of Arksey were turning their attentions to the church. Dr Burrows, the Bishop of the Diocese, dedicated two bells that had been added to the peal of six that were already in the church tower. One of the bells was dedicated to the memory of those men who belonged to the parish who had fallen in the Great War and the other in commemoration of Peace. There was a tablet bearing the names of the fallen, the renovated clock and the Cambridge full quarter chimes that had been gifted by Miss Dunhill of Coney Garth, one of the churchwardens, in memory of her late parents. There was a Litany desk given by the Vicar, the Reverend A. Rhys-James, in memory of his two children who died in the parish, and a Litany service book given by Mrs Thompson in memory of her late husband, Charles Clifford Thompson, a former organist of the church.

The inscription on one of the new bells reads, 'In Memory of the Fallen 1914-1919', and on the other, 'Peace after Victory 1919'. On the tablet, the names that appeared were Herbert Hopper, Jim Leeking, W. Leadbeater, Alfred Leadbeater, Charles Leadbeater, Charles Webster, Robert Norris, Charles Arrand, Harry Frost, John William Dawson, George Arthur, Stanley Hirst, Henry Severn - R.I.P'. After the service a parish tea was provided in the grounds of Arksey Hall by kind permission of Mr Nuttall where the Bishop and his wife visited the grounds and chatted with the people.

Although the War had ended and the Armistice signed some months ago, many local men were still abroad as part of an army of occupation, policing the war zones and battlefields at the transition between hostility and peace. The true, symbolic end of the horrific affair had to be on the occasion when the 1/5th KOYLI were welcomed home for good by way of a service of thanksgiving held at the Parish Church. The service was also attended by the Mayor and Corporation where Archdeacon Sandford gave an eloquent address, highlighting the fine work of the battalion and paying tribute to those who had laid down their lives. At the conclusion of the service, lunch was served at the Mansion House to past and present officers.

The procession to the church was headed by the Territorial Band followed closely by the Mayor, Councillor R.M. Jackson, the Mayor of Pontefract, Alderman Sides, the Chairmen of the Goole, Featherstone and Castleford Urban District Councils, and several members of the Town Council and officials, including Mr Tovey, the Town Clerk. There were well known officers present too, namely, Colonel Moxon CMG DSO, Commander of 5th KOYLI, Lieutenant Colonel Parkin DSO, Lieutenant Colonel E. Bernard Wilson DSO formerly CO of 5th Battalion KOYLI, Major Sullivan MC, Adjutant and Major Shearman DSO, among a great many other distinguished officers. There were two colour bearers along with the battalion's VC hero, Sergeant Calvert. The pulpit at the church was draped with the Union Flag and the Colours of the regiment were placed in the nave. Archdeacon Sandford said:

'We welcome you with full hearts and open arms on making their official return to the depot of their gallant battalion. You went out to fight a great battle for truth, righteousness, and freedom and you have come back crowned with victory. We have gathered here today to thank God for that victory. The people of Doncaster are grateful to you for all you have done and you have every reason to be proud of yourselves. You will not be forgotten and we will never forget the splendid service you have rendered. The people of Doncaster are proud to know that they are the fathers, brothers, and friends of such a gallant army of men such as you. We think of those men that have lost their lives in this with love and affection, how can we think of them except with deep reverence and profound devotion? We wanted you to go at the first call, and when some of you fell our hearts were nearly broken. Let those who fought for truth, righteousness, and justice, fight for it at home all your lives long in order that we might make Doncaster a better Doncaster than ever.'

As we today gather at our respective war memorials on the eleventh hour of the eleventh day of the eleventh month, in order to honour those who fell in that Great War along with every other war since then, let us think back to that very first official day of remembrance when the pain of the greatest war that this country had ever known was still heartbreakingly fresh in every Doncastrian's mind. At eleven o'clock on 11 November 1919, at Clock Corner in Doncaster a very large crowd had gathered to watch each other stand still and to witness the stationary traffic. All eyes were fixed on the clock, and in a silence that became more and more impressive as the minutes ticked by, the hands at length pointed to eleven. Then, from far down the street came the mellow, plaintive notes of the 'Last Post', so full of melody and so full of meaning. Trams stopped, motorcars pulled up, and everybody stood

War Memorial at St Mary's Church, Sprotbrough
©www.doncasterhistory.co.uk

Gathering crowd at Clock Corner.

still and remained silent as the grave. A clattering van in the French Gate district was stopped by the upraised hand of a police sergeant while the two minutes silence was rigidly observed. It was tense while it lasted. The meaning of it, and recollections, brought tears to the eyes of many and even strong men were seen to produce handkerchiefs and apply them to their weeping eyes.

It is my hope that this book, and particularly these final few words, bring a new pride and meaning to successive Remembrance Day proceedings. Lest We Forget.

Private Harold Smith KOYLI, Killed
©Jane Petch 2013

Gv R I

HE whom this scroll commemorates was numbered among those who, at the call of King and Country, left all that was dear to them, endured hardness, faced danger, and finally passed out of the sight of men by the path of duty and self-sacrifice, giving up their own lives that others might live in freedom. Let those who come after see to it that his name be not forgotten.

Pte: Harold Smith
Yorkshire L. I.

Private Harold Smith's Scroll ©Jane Petch 2013

Rifleman George W. Wyatt, and his Death
Penny ©Rob Burns 2013

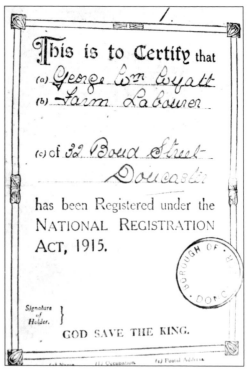

Soldier's Keepsake complete with French battlefield mud ©Rob Burns 2013

National Registration Certificate ©Rob Burns 2013

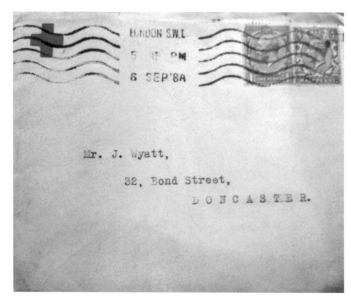

The Dreaded Letter ©Rob Burns 2013

Overseas Club Certificate
1915 ©Barry Morgan
2013

Private Samuel Sutcliffe
©Margaret Herbert
2013

One of the luckiest families in Doncaster, five sons went to war and all five came back alive. Back Row L-R, Albert Edward Needham, Tom Needham, Harry Needham, Charles Needham. Front Row L-R, David Needham jnr, Inspector David Needham Borough Police, Ellis Needham. ©Margaret Herbert 2013

Soldiers encamped at Doncaster.

QOYD Parade, Bennetthorpe.

Bibliography

Halifax, Earl of (1957). *Fullness of Days* London; Collins

Oakes, Geoffrey (1995). *Aviation in Doncaster 1909-1992,* Doncaster, G.H. Oakes

Lockhart, J.G. (1935). *Viscount Halifax 1839-1885,* London, Geoffrey Bles

Laffin, John (1985). *On the Western Front 1914-1918,* Gloucester, Alan Sutton Publishing Ltd.

List of Illustrations

Index